Chicago White Sox 2021

A Baseball Companion

Edited by Steven Goldman and Bret Sayre

Baseball Prospectus

Craig Brown, Associate Editor
Robert Au, Harry Pavlidis and Amy Pircher, Statistics Editors

Copyright © 2021 by DIY Baseball, LLC.
All rights reserved

This book or any part thereof may not be reproduced or transmitted in any form or by any means, electronic or mechanical, including photocopying, recording, or by any information storage and retrieval system, without permission in writing from the publisher.

Limit of Liability/Disclaimer of Warranty: While the publisher and the author have used their best efforts in preparing this book, they make no representations or warranties with respect to the accuracy or completeness of the contents of this book and specifically disclaim any implied warranties of merchantability or fitness for a particular purpose. No warranty may be created or extended by sales representatives or written sales materials. The advice and strategies contained herein may not be suitable for your situation. You should consult with a professional where appropriate. Neither the publisher nor the author shall be liable for any loss of profit or any other commercial damages, including but not limited to special, incidental, consequential, or other damages.

Library of Congress Cataloging-in-Publication Data:
paperback
ISBN-13: 978-1-950716-35-7

Project Credits
Cover Design: Ginny Searle
Interior Design and Production: Amy Pircher, Robert Au
Layout: Amy Pircher, Robert Au

Baseball icon courtesy of Uberux, from https://www.shareicon.net/author/uberux

Ballpark diagram courtesy of Lou Spirito/THIRTY81 Project, https://thirty81project.com/

Manufactured in the United States of America
10 9 8 7 6 5 4 3 2 1

Table of Contents

Statistical Introduction v

Part 1: Team Analysis
Performance Graphs 3
2020 Team Performance 4
2021 Team Projections 5
Team Personnel 6
Guaranteed Rate Field Stats 7
White Sox Team Analysis 9

Part 2: Player Analysis
White Sox Player Analysis 14
White Sox Prospects 83

Part 3: Featured Articles
White Sox All-Time Top 10 Players 95
    by Rob Mains
A Taxonomy of 2020 Abnormalities 101
    by Rob Mains
Tranches of WAR 107
    by Russell A. Carleton
Secondhand Sport 113
    by Patrick Dubuque
Steve Dalkowski Dreaming 117
    by Steven Goldman
A Reward For A Functioning Society 121
    by Cory Frontin and Craig Goldstein

Index of Names 125

Statistical Introduction

Sports are, fundamentally, a blend of athletic endeavor and storytelling. Baseball, like any other sport, tells its stories in so many ways: in the arc of a game from the stands or a season from the box scores, in photos, or even in numbers. At Baseball Prospectus, we understand that statistics don't replace observation or any of baseball's stories, but complement everything else that makes the game so much fun.

What stats help us with is with patterns and precision, variance and value. This book can help you learn things you may not see from watching a game or hundred, whether it's the path of a career over time or the breadth of the entire MLB. We'd also never ask you to choose between our numbers and the experience of viewing a game from the cheap seats or the comfort of your home; our publication combines running the numbers with observations and wisdom from some of the brightest minds we can find. But if you *do* want to learn more about the numbers beyond what's on the backs of player jerseys, let us help explain.

Offense

We've revised our methodology for determining batting value. Long-time readers of the book will notice that we've retired True Average in favor of a new metric: Deserved Runs Created Plus (DRC+). Developed by Jonathan Judge and our stats team, this statistic measures everything a player does at the plate–reaching base, hitting for power, making outs, and moving runners over–and puts it on a scale where 100 equals league-average performance. A DRC+ of 150 is terrific, a DRC+ of 100 is average and a DRC+ of 75 means you better be an excellent defender.

DRC+ also does a better job than any of our previous metrics in taking contextual factors into account. The model adjusts for how the park affects performance, but also for things like the talent of the opposing pitcher, value of different types of batted-ball events, league, temperature and other factors. It's able to describe a player's expected offensive contribution than any other statistic we've found over the years, and also does a better job of predicting future performance as well.

The other aspect of run-scoring is baserunning, which we quantify using Baserunning Runs. BRR not only records the value of stolen bases (or getting caught in the act), but also accounts for all the stuff that doesn't show up on the back of a baseball card: a runner's ability to go first to third on a single, or advance on a fly ball.

Defense

Where offensive value is *relatively* easy to identify and understand, defensive value is ... not. Over the past dozen years, the sabermetric community has focused mostly on stats based on zone data: a real-live human person records the type of batted ball and estimated landing location, and models are created that give expected outs. From there, you can compare fielders' actual outs to those expected ones. Simple, right?

Unfortunately, zone data has two major issues. First, zone data is recorded by commercial data providers who keep the raw data private unless you pay for it. (All the statistics we build in this book and on our website use public data as inputs.) That hurts our ability to test assumptions or duplicate results. Second, over the years it has become apparent that there's quite a bit of "noise" in zone-based fielding analysis. Sometimes the conclusions drawn from zone data don't hold up to scrutiny, and sometimes the different data provided by different providers don't look anything alike, giving wildly different results. Sometimes the hard-working professional stringers or scorers might unknowingly inflict unconscious bias into the mix: for example good fielders will often be credited with more expected outs despite the data, and ballparks with high press boxes tend to score more line drives than ones with a lower press box.

Enter our Fielding Runs Above Average (FRAA). For most positions, FRAA is built from play-by-play data, which allows us to avoid the subjectivity found in many other fielding metrics. The idea is this: count how many fielding plays are made by a given player and compare that to expected plays for an average fielder at their position (based on pitcher ground ball tendencies and batter handedness). Then we adjust for park and base-out situations.

When it comes to catchers, our methodology is a little different thanks to the laundry list of responsibilities they're tasked with beyond just, well, catching and throwing the ball. By now you've probably heard about "framing" or the art of making umpires more likely to call balls outside the strike zone for strikes. To put this into one tidy number, we incorporate pitch tracking data (for the years it exists) and adjust for important factors like pitcher, umpire, batter and home-field advantage using a mixed-model approach. This grants us a number for how many strikes the catcher is personally adding to (or subtracting from) his pitchers' performance ... which we then convert to runs added or lost using linear weights.

Framing is one of the biggest parts of determining catcher value, but we also take into account blocking balls from going past, whether a scorer deems it a passed ball or a wild pitch. We use a similar approach—one that really benefits from the pitch tracking data that tells us what ends up in the dirt and what doesn't. We also include a catcher's ability to prevent stolen bases and how well they field balls in play, and *finally* we come up with our FRAA for catchers.

Pitching

Both pitching and fielding make up the half of baseball that isn't run scoring: run prevention. Separating pitching from fielding is a tough task, and most recent pitching analysis has branched off from Voros McCracken's famous (and controversial) statement, "There is little if any difference among major-league pitchers in their ability to prevent hits on balls hit in the field of play." The research of the analytic community has validated this to some extent, and there are a host of "defense-independent" pitching measures that have been developed to try and extract the effect of the defense behind a hurler from the pitcher's work.

Our solution to this quandary is Deserved Run Average (DRA), our core pitching metric. DRA seeks to evaluate a pitcher's performance, much like earned run average (ERA), the tried-and-true pitching stat you've seen on every baseball broadcast or box score from the past century, but it's very different. To start, DRA takes an event-by-event look at what the pitchers does, and adjusts the value of that event based on different environmental factors like park, batter, catcher, umpire, base-out situation, run differential, inning, defense, home field advantage, pitcher role and temperature. That mixed model gives us a pitcher's expected contribution, similar to what we do for our DRC+ model for hitters and FRAA model for catchers. (Oh, and we also consider the pitcher's effect on basestealing and on balls getting past the catcher.)

DRA is set to the scale of runs allowed per nine innings (RA9) instead of ERA, which makes DRA's scale slightly higher than ERA's. Because of this, for ease of use, we're supplying DRA-, which is much easier for the reader to parse. As with DRC+, DRA- is an "index" stat, meaning instead of using some arbitrary and shifting number to denote what's "good," average is always 100. The reason that it uses a minus rather than a plus is because like ERA, a lower number is better. Therefore a 75 DRA- describes a performance 25 percent better than average, whereas a 150 DRA- means that either a pitcher is getting extremely lucky with their results, or getting ready to try a new pitch.

Since the last time you picked up an edition of this book, we've also made a few minor changes to DRA to make it better. Recent research into "tunneling"—the act of throwing consecutive pitches that appear similar from a batter's point of view until after the swing decision point–data has given us a new contextual factor to account for in DRA: plate distance. This refers to the distance between successive pitches as they approach the plate, and while it has a smaller effect than factors like velocity or whiff rate, it still can help explain pitcher strikeout rate in our model.

Recently Added Descriptive Statistics

Returning to our 2021 edition of the book are a few figures which recently appeared. These numbers may be a little bit more familiar to those of you who have spent some time investigating baseball statistics.

Fastball Percentage

Our fastball percentage (FA%) statistic measures how frequently a pitcher throws a pitch classified as a "fastball," measured as a percentage of overall pitches thrown. We qualify three types of fastballs:

1. The traditional four-seam fastball;
2. The two-seam fastball or sinker;
3. "Hard cutters," which are pitches that have the movement profile of a cut fastball and are used as the pitcher's primary offering or in place of a more traditional fastball.

For example, a pitcher with a FA% of 67 throws any combination of these three pitches about two-thirds of the time.

Whiff Rate

Everybody loves a swing and a miss, and whiff rate (Whiff%) measures how frequently pitchers induce a swinging strike. To calculate Whiff%, we add up all the pitches thrown that ended with a swinging strike, then divide that number by a pitcher's total pitches thrown. Most often, high whiff rates correlate with high strikeout rates (and overall effective pitcher performance).

Called Strike Probability

Called Strike Probability (CSP) is a number that represents the likelihood that all of a pitcher's pitches will be called a strike while controlling for location, pitcher and batter handedness, umpire and count. Here's how it works: on each pitch, our model determines how many times (out of 100) that a similar pitch was called for a strike given those factors mentioned above, and when normalized for each batter's strike zone. Then we average the CSP for all pitches thrown by a pitcher in a season, and that gives us the yearly CSP percentage you see in the stats boxes.

As you might imagine, pitchers with a higher CSP are more likely to work in the zone, where pitchers with a lower CSP are likely locating their pitches outside the normal strike zone, for better or for worse.

Projections

Many of you aren't turning to this book just for a look at what a player has done, but for a look at what a player is going to do: the PECOTA projections. PECOTA, initially developed by Nate Silver (who has moved on to greater fame as a political analyst), consists of three parts:

1. Major-league equivalencies, which use minor-league statistics to project how a player will perform in the major leagues;
2. Baseline forecasts, which use weighted averages and regression to the mean to estimate a player's current true talent level; and
3. Aging curves, which uses the career paths of comparable players to estimate how a player's statistics are likely to change over time.

With all those important things covered, let's take a look at what's in the book this year.

Team Prospectus

Most of this book is composed of team chapters, with one for each of the 30 major-league franchises. On the first page of each chapter, you'll see a box that contains some of the key statistics for each team as well as a very inviting stadium diagram.

We start with the team name, their unadjusted 2020 win-loss record, and their divisional ranking. Beneath that are a host of other team statistics. **Pythag** presents an adjusted 2020 winning percentage, calculated by taking runs scored per game (**RS/G**) and runs allowed per game (**RA/G**) for the team, and running them through a version of Bill James' Pythagorean formula that was refined and improved by David Smyth and Brandon Heipp. (The formula is called "Pythagenpat," which is equally fun to type and to say.)

Next up is **DRC+**, described earlier, to indicate the overall hitting ability of the team either above or below league-average. Run prevention on the pitching side is covered by **DRA** (also mentioned earlier) and another metric: Fielding Independent Pitching (**FIP**), which calculates another ERA-like statistic based on strikeouts, walks, and home runs recorded. Defensive Efficiency Rating (**DER**) tells us the percentage of balls in play turned into outs for the team, and is a quick fielding shorthand that rounds out run prevention.

After that, we have several measures related to roster composition, as opposed to on-field performance. **B-Age** and **P-Age** tell us the average age of a team's batters and pitchers, respectively. **Payroll** is the combined team payroll for all on-field players, and Doug Pappas' Marginal Dollars per Marginal Win (**M$/MW**) tells us how much money a team spent to earn production above replacement level.

Next to each of these stats, we've listed each team's MLB rank in that category from first to 30th. In this, first always indicates a positive outcome and 30th a negative outcome, except in the case of salary—first is highest.

After the franchise statistics, we share a few items about the team's home ballpark. There's the aforementioned diagram of the park's dimensions (including distances to the outfield wall), a graphic showing the height of the wall from the left-field pole to the right-field pole, and a table showing three-year park factors for the stadium. The park factors are displayed as indexes where 100 is average, 110 means that the park inflates the statistic in question by 10 percent, and 90 means that the park deflates the statistic in question by 10 percent.

On the second page of each team chapter, you'll find three graphs. The first is **Payroll History** and helps you see how the team's payroll has compared to the MLB and divisional average payrolls over time. Payroll figures are current as of January 1, 2021; with so many free agents still unsigned as of this writing, the final 2021 figure will likely be significantly different for many teams. (In the meantime, you can always find the most current data at Baseball Prospectus' Cot's Baseball Contracts page.)

The second graph is **Future Commitments** and helps you see the team's future outlays, if any.

The third graph is **Farm System Ranking** and displays how the Baseball Prospectus prospect team has ranked the organization's farm system since 2007.

After the graphs, we have a **Personnel** section that lists many of the important decision-makers and upper-level field and operations staff members for the franchise, as well as any former Baseball Prospectus staff members who are currently part of the organization. (In very rare circumstances, someone might be on both lists!)

Position Players

After all that information and a thoughtful bylined essay covering each team, we present our player comments. These are also bylined, but due to frequent franchise shifts during the offseason, our bylines are more a rough guide than a perfect accounting of who wrote what.

Each player is listed with the major-league team that employed him as of early January 2021. If a player changed teams after that point via free agency, trade, or any other method, you'll be able to find them in the chapter for their previous squad.

As an example, take a look at the player comment for Padres shortstop Fernando Tatis Jr.: the stat block that accompanies his written comment is at the top of this page. First we cover biographical information (age is as of June 30, 2021) before moving onto the stats themselves. Our statistic columns include standard identifying information like **YEAR**, **TEAM**, **LVL** (level of affiliated play) and **AGE** before getting into the numbers. Next, we provide raw, untranslated

Fernando Tatis Jr. SS
Born: 01/02/99 Age: 22 Bats: R Throws: R
Height: 6'3" Weight: 217 Origin: International Free Agent, 2015

YEAR	TEAM	LVL	AGE	PA	R	2B	3B	HR	RBI	BB	K	SB	CS	AVG/OBP/SLG
2018	SA	AA	19	394	77	22	4	16	43	33	109	16	5	.286/.355/.507
2019	SD	MLB	20	372	61	13	6	22	53	30	110	16	6	.317/.379/.590
2020	SD	MLB	21	257	50	11	2	17	45	27	61	11	3	.277/.366/.571
2021 FS	SD	MLB	22	600	95	24	4	31	81	50	165	17	8	.263/.331/.499
2021 DC	SD	MLB	22	628	100	25	4	32	85	53	173	19	8	.263/.331/.499

Comparables: Darryl Strawberry, Bo Bichette, Ronald Acuña Jr.

YEAR	TEAM	LVL	AGE	PA	DRC+	BABIP	BRR	FRAA	WARP
2018	SA	AA	19	394	136	.370	3.0	SS(83): -1.9	2.4
2019	SD	MLB	20	372	118	.410	7.1	SS(83): 0.9	3.4
2020	SD	MLB	21	257	126	.306	0.7	SS(57): -5.5	0.9
2021 FS	SD	MLB	22	600	126	.318	1.7	SS -1	3.9
2021 DC	SD	MLB	22	628	126	.318	1.8	SS -1	4.0

numbers like you might find on the back of your dad's baseball cards: **PA** (plate appearances), **R** (runs), **2B** (doubles), **3B** (triples), **HR** (home runs), **RBI** (runs batted in), **BB** (walks), **K** (strikeouts), **SB** (stolen bases) and **CS** (caught stealing).

Following the basic stats is **Whiff%** (whiff rate), which denotes how often, when a batter swings, he fails to make contact with the ball. Another way to think of this number is an inverse of a hitter's contact rate.

Next, we have unadjusted "slash" statistics: **AVG** (batting average), **OBP** (on-base percentage) and **SLG** (slugging percentage). Following the slash line is **DRC+** (Deserved Runs Created Plus), which we described earlier as total offensive expected contribution compared to the league average.

BABIP (batting average on balls in play) tells us how often a ball in play fell for a hit, and can help us identify whether a batter may have been lucky or not ... but note that high BABIPs also tend to follow the great hitters of our time, as well as speedy singles hitters who put the ball on the ground.

The next item is **BRR** (Baserunning Runs), which covers all of a player's baserunning accomplishments including (but not limited to) swiped bags and failed attempts. Next is **FRAA** (Fielding Runs Above Average), which also includes the number of games previously played at each position noted in parentheses. Multi-position players have only their two most frequent positions listed here, but their total FRAA number reflects all positions played.

Our last column here is **WARP** (Wins Above Replacement Player). WARP estimates the total value of a player, which means for hitters it takes into account hitting runs above average (calculated using the DRC+ model), BRR and FRAA. Then, it makes an adjustment for positions played and gives the player a credit

Chicago White Sox 2021

for plate appearances based upon the difference between "replacement level"—which is derived from the quality of players added to a team's roster after the start of the season–and the league average.

The final line just below the stats box is **PECOTA** data, which is discussed further in a following section.

Catchers

Catchers are a special breed, and thus they have earned their own separate box which displays some of the defensive metrics that we've built just for them. As an example, let's check out Yasmani Grandal.

YEAR	TEAM	P. COUNT	FRM RUNS	BLK RUNS	THRW RUNS	TOT RUNS
2018	LAD	16816	15.7	0.8	0.1	16.5
2019	MIL	18740	19.4	1.8	-0.1	21.1
2020	CHW	4830	3.7	0.3	-0.2	3.8
2021	CHW	14430	16.7	-0.6	1.0	17.1
2021	CHW	14430	16.7	0.4	1.0	18.0

The **YEAR** and **TEAM** columns match what you'd find in the other stat box. **P. COUNT** indicates the number of pitches thrown while the catcher was behind the plate, including swinging strikes, fouls and balls in play. **FRM RUNS** is the total run value the catcher provided (or cost) his team by influencing the umpire to call strikes where other catchers did not. **BLK RUNS** expresses the total run value above or below average for the catcher's ability to prevent wild pitches and passed balls. **THRW RUNS** is calculated using a similar model as the previous two statistics, and it measures a catcher's ability to throw out basestealers but also to dissuade them from testing his arm in the first place. It takes into account factors like the pitcher (including his delivery and pickoff move) and baserunner (who could be as fast as Billy Hamilton or as slow as Yonder Alonso). **TOT RUNS** is the sum of all of the previous three statistics.

Pitchers

Let's give our pitchers a turn, using 2020 AL Cy Young winner Shane Bieber as our example. Take a look at his stat block: the first line and the **YEAR**, **TEAM**, **LVL** and **AGE** columns are the same as in the position player example earlier.

Here too, we have a series of columns that display raw, unadjusted statistics compiled by the pitcher over the course of a season: **W** (wins), **L** (losses), **SV** (saves), **G** (games pitched), **GS** (games started), **IP** (innings pitched), **H** (hits allowed) and **HR** (home runs allowed). Next we have two statistics that are rates: **BB/9** (walks per nine innings) and **K/9** (strikeouts per nine innings), before returning to the unadjusted **K** (strikeouts).

Next up is **GB%** (ground ball percentage), which is the percentage of all batted balls that were hit on the ground, including both outs and hits. Remember, this is based on observational data and subject to human error, so please approach this with a healthy dose of skepticism.

BABIP (batting average on balls in play) is calculated using the same methodology as it is for position players, but it often tells us more about a pitcher than it does a hitter. With pitchers, a high BABIP is often due to poor defense or bad luck, and can often be an indicator of potential rebound, and a low BABIP may be cause to expect performance regression. (A typical league-average BABIP is close to .290-.300.)

The metrics **WHIP** (walks plus hits per inning pitched) and **ERA** (earned run average) are old standbys: WHIP measures walks and hits allowed on a per-inning basis, while ERA measures earned runs on a nine-inning basis. Neither of these stats are translated or adjusted.

DRA- (Deserved Run Average) was described at length earlier, and measures how the pitcher "deserved" to perform compared to other pitchers. Please note that since we lack all the data points that would make for a "real" DRA for minor-league events, the DRA- displayed for minor league partial-seasons is based off of different data. (That data is a modified version of our cFIP metric, which you can find more information about on our website.)

Shane Bieber   RHP
Born: 05/31/95   Age: 26   Bats: R   Throws: R
Height: 6'3"   Weight: 200   Origin: Round 4, 2016 Draft (#122 overall)

YEAR	TEAM	LVL	AGE	W	L	SV	G	GS	IP	H	HR	BB/9	K/9	K	GB%	BABIP
2018	AKR	AA	23	3	0	0	5	5	31	26	1	0.3	8.7	30	47.3%	.278
2018	COL	AAA	23	3	1	0	8	8	48^2	30	3	1.1	8.7	47	52.0%	.227
2018	CLE	MLB	23	11	5	0	20	19	114^2	130	13	1.8	9.3	118	46.2%	.356
2019	CLE	MLB	24	15	8	0	34	33	214^1	186	31	1.7	10.9	259	44.4%	.298
2020	CLE	MLB	25	8	1	0	12	12	77^1	46	7	2.4	14.2	122	48.4%	.267
2021 FS	CLE	MLB	26	10	6	0	26	26	150	121	18	2.1	11.7	195	45.5%	.297
2021 DC	CLE	MLB	26	14	7	0	30	30	196.7	159	24	2.1	11.7	257	45.5%	.297

Comparables: Luis Severino, Danny Salazar, Joe Musgrove

YEAR	TEAM	LVL	AGE	WHIP	ERA	DRA-	WARP	MPH	FB%	WHF	CSP
2018	AKR	AA	23	0.87	1.16	61	0.9				
2018	COL	AAA	23	0.74	1.66	69	1.2				
2018	CLE	MLB	23	1.33	4.55	74	2.6	94.7	57.4%	26.2%	
2019	CLE	MLB	24	1.05	3.28	75	4.9	94.4	45.8%	30.8%	
2020	CLE	MLB	25	0.87	1.63	53	2.6	95.3	53.6%	40.7%	
2021 FS	CLE	MLB	26	1.04	2.44	64	4.4	94.7	50.0%	33.2%	44.2%
2021 DC	CLE	MLB	26	1.04	2.44	64	5.8	94.7	50.0%	33.2%	44.2%

Just like with hitters, **WARP** (Wins Above Replacement Player) is a total value metric that puts pitchers of all stripes on the same scale as position players. We use DRA as the primary input for our calculation of WARP. You might notice that relief pitchers (due to their limited innings) may have a lower WARP than you were expecting or than you might see in other WARP-like metrics. WARP does not take leverage into account, just the actions a pitcher performs and the expected value of those actions ... which ends up judging high-leverage relief pitchers differently than you might imagine given their prestige and market value.

MPH gives you the pitcher's 95th percentile velocity for the noted season, in order to give you an idea of what the *peak* fastball velocity a pitcher possesses. Since this comes from our pitch-tracking data, it is not publicly available for minor-league pitchers.

Finally, we display the three new pitching metrics we described earlier. **FB%** (fastball percentage) gives you the percentage of fastballs thrown out of all pitches. **WHF** (whiff rate) tells you the percentage of swinging strikes induced out of all pitches. **CSP** (called strike probability) expresses the likelihood of all pitches thrown to result in a called strike, after controlling for factors like handedness, umpire, pitch type, count and location.

PECOTA

All players have PECOTA projections for 2021, as well as a set of other numbers that describe the performance of comparable players according to PECOTA. All projections for 2021 are for the player at the date we went to press in early January and are projected into the league and park context as indicated by the team abbreviation. (Note that players at very low levels of the minors are too unpredictable to assess using these numbers.) All PECOTA projected statistics represent a player's projected major-league performance.

How we're doing that is a little different this season. There are really two different values that go into the final stat line that you see for PECOTA: How a player performs, and how much playing time he'll be given to perform it. In the past we've estimated playing time based on each team's roster and depth charts, and we'll continue to do that. These projections are denoted as **2021 DC**.

But in many cases, a player won't be projected for major-league playing time; most of the time this is because they aren't projected to be major-league players at all, but still developing as prospects. Or perhaps a player will provide Triple-A depth, only to have an opportunity open up because of injury. For these purposes, we're also supplying a second projection, labeled **2021 FS**, or full season. This is what we would project the player to provide in 600 plate appearances or 150 innings pitched.

Below the projections are the player's three highest-scoring comparable players as determined by PECOTA. All comparables represent a snapshot of how the listed player was performing at the same age as the current player, so if a

23-year-old pitcher is compared to Bartolo Colón, he's actually being compared to a 23-year-old Colón, not the version that pitched for the Rangers in 2018, nor to Colón's career as a whole.

A few points about pitcher projections. First, we aren't yet projecting peak velocity, so that column will be blank in the PECOTA lines. Second, projecting DRA is trickier than evaluating past performance, because it is unclear how deserving each pitcher will be of his anticipated outcomes. However, we know that another DRA-related statistic–contextual FIP or cFIP–estimates future run scoring very well. So for PECOTA, the projected DRA- figures you see are based on the past cFIPs generated by the pitcher and comparable players over time, along with the other factors described above.

If you're familiar with PECOTA, then you'll have noticed that the projection system often appears bullish on players coming off a bad year and bearish on players coming off a good year. (This is because the system weights several previous seasons, not just the most recent one.) In addition, we publish the 50th percentile projections for each player–which is smack in the middle of the range of projected production—which tends to mean PECOTA stat lines don't often have extreme results like 40 home runs or 250 strikeouts in a given season. In essence, PECOTA doesn't project very many extreme seasons.

Managers

After all those wonderful team chapters, we've got statistics for each big-league manager, all of whom are organized by alphabetical order. Here you'll find a block including an extraordinary amount of information collected from each manager's entire career. For more information on the acronyms and what they mean, please visit the Glossary at www.baseballprospectus.com.

There is one important metric that we'd like to call attention to, and you'll find it next to each manager's name: **wRM+** (weighted reliever management plus). Developed by Rob Arthur and Rian Watt, wRM+ investigates how good a manager is at using their best relievers during the moments of highest leverage, using both our proprietary DRA metric as well as Leverage Index. wRM+ is scaled to a league average of 100, and a wRM+ of 105 indicates that relievers were used approximately five percent "better" than average. On the other hand, a wRM+ of 95 would tell us the team used its relievers five percent "worse" than the average team.

While wRM+ does not have an extremely strong correlation with a manager, it is statistically significant; this means that a manager is not *entirely* responsible for a team's wRM+, but does have some effect on that number.

Part 1: Team Analysis

Performance Graphs

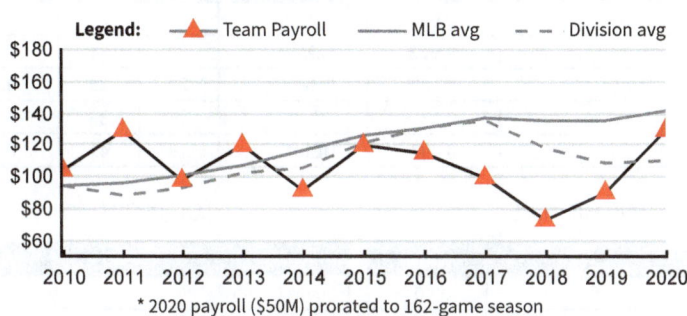

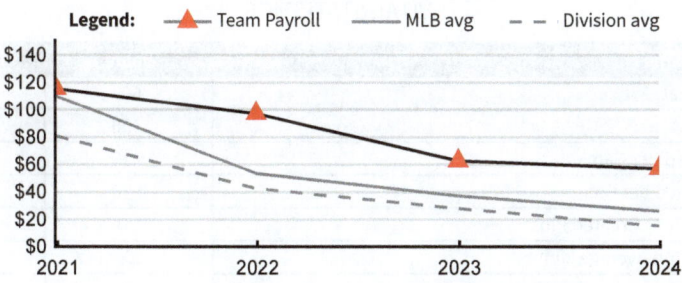

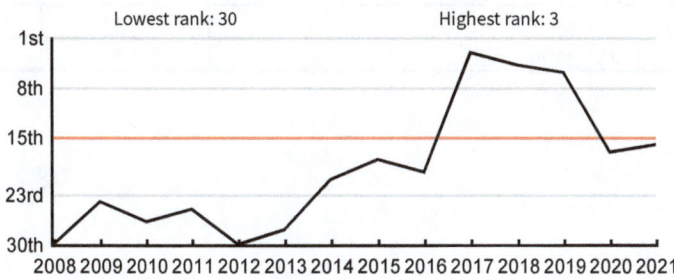

2020 Team Performance

ACTUAL STANDINGS

Team	W	L	Pct
MIN	36	24	0.600
CHW	**35**	**25**	**0.583**
CLE	35	25	0.583
KC	26	34	0.433
DET	23	35	0.397

dWIN% STANDINGS

Team	W	L	Pct
CLE	30	30	0.506
MIN	29	31	0.498
CHW	**27**	**33**	**0.456**
KC	24	36	0.403
DET	19	41	0.333

TOP HITTERS

Player	WARP
José Abreu	2.0
Luis Robert	1.4
Yasmani Grandal	1.2

TOP PITCHERS

Player	WARP
Lucas Giolito	1.6
Evan Marshall	0.6
Dallas Keuchel	0.6

VITAL STATISTICS

Statistic Name	Value	Rank
Pythagenpat	.602	4th
dWin%	.456	17th
Runs Scored per Game	5.10	5th
Runs Allowed per Game	4.10	10th
Deserved Runs Created Plus	101	15th
Deserved Run Average Minus	102	19th
Fielding Independent Pitching	4.37	12th
Defensive Efficiency Rating	.715	3rd
Batter Age	28.1	10th
Pitcher Age	28.2	11th
Payroll	$50.0M	20th
Marginal $ per Marginal Win	$1.9M	7th

2021 Team Projections

PROJECTED STANDINGS

Team	W	L	Pct	+/-
MIN	90.8	71.2	0.560	-6
With Nelson Cruz returning and Andrelton Simmons, J.A. Happ, and Alex Colomé on board the Twins seem like a balanced behemoth again.			
CLE	85.0	77.0	0.525	-9
That they've lost so many great players is an indictment of ownership. That they remain respectable is a testament to the agility of the front office.			
CHW	82.8	79.2	0.511	-11
Lance Lynn and Liam Hendriks give Tony La Russa the paint-by-numbers pitching staff he prefers, and all of the crucial cogs in last year's young lineup return.			
KC	71.5	90.5	0.441	1
Creeping back toward respectability, the Royals added reliable veterans coming off down years and will hope their youth movement gains momentum quickly.			
DET	65.7	96.3	0.406	3
The trend arrow is finally pointing up, but Robbie Grossman and Wilson Ramos qualifying as significant improvements shows they still have a long way to go.			

TOP PROJECTED HITTERS

Player	WARP
Yasmani Grandal	4.2
Eloy Jiménez	3.1
Luis Robert	2.4

TOP PROJECTED PITCHERS

Player	WARP
Lucas Giolito	3.3
Lance Lynn	2.7
Dallas Keuchel	2.1

FARM SYSTEM REPORT

Top Prospect	Number of Top 101 Prospects
Nick Madrigal, #12	4

KEY DEDUCTIONS

Player	WARP
Dane Dunning	1.5
James McCann	1.0
Yolmer Sánchez	0.7
Alex Colomé	0.4
Nomar Mazara	0.3

KEY ADDITIONS

Player	WARP
Lance Lynn	2.7
Adam Eaton	1.6
Liam Hendriks	1.4
Michael Kopech	0.7

Team Personnel

Executive Vice President
Ken Williams

Senior Vice President/General Manager
Rick Hahn

Assistant General Manager
Jeremy Haber

Senior Director of Baseball Operations
Dan Fabian

Director of Player Development
Chris Getz

Manager
Tony LaRussa

BP Alumni
Steffan Segui

Guaranteed Rate Field Stats

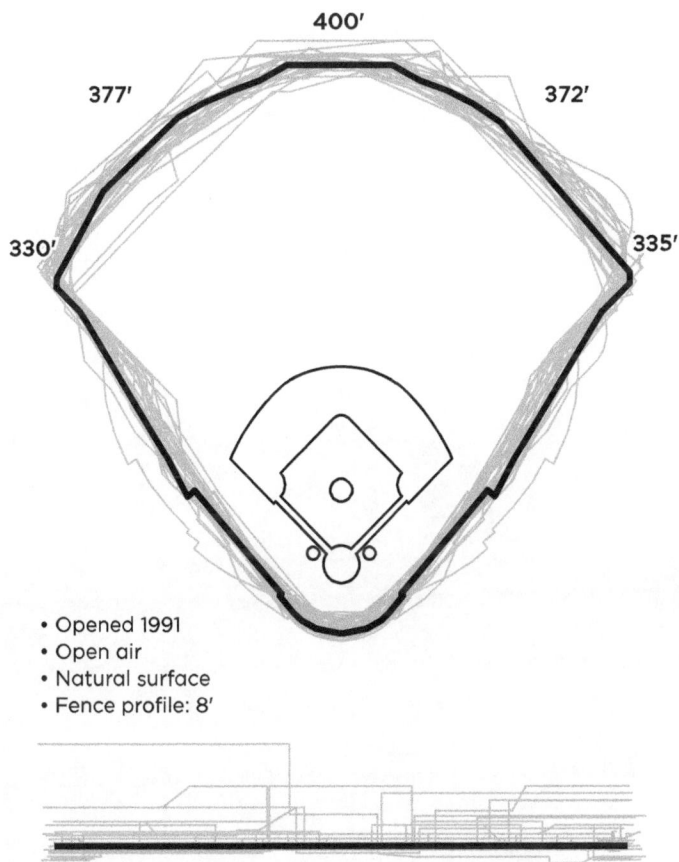

- Opened 1991
- Open air
- Natural surface
- Fence profile: 8'

Three-Year Park Factors

Runs	Runs/RH	Runs/LH	HR/RH	HR/LH
98	97	100	103	113

White Sox Team Analysis

Emotions overcame José Abreu on November 12, when informed that he had been voted the American League Most Valuable Player. Abreu was at a loss of words at first. It was a major accomplishment for "Pito," the Cuban native's family nickname. He composed himself after about a minute. Then he shared why he pointed to a photo of his grandmother, who had been one of Abreu's lifelong supporters but had recently died. Joy mixed with grief. It was a combination that would become familiar to many in 2020.

In winning the 2020 AL MVP Award Abreu became the first Cuban baseball defector to earn the title in the majors. His story is quite different than the other two Cuban-born MVP winners. Fellow AL MVPs Zoilo Versalles (1965) and José Canseco (1988) were both born in Cuba, but they were not defectors in the same sense as Abreu. The Sox first baseman left his native land after becoming a standout in Cuba's National Series.

Abreu's award-winning season was a major part of the 2020 White Sox success. Just as notable, he was his part of the distinct Latino flavor of the Southside squad. The team featured Latinos from across the Americas all around the diamond, from the infield to the outfield, the starting rotation and bullpen, and at the managerial helm.

Managing the Southsiders

The Southsiders made the playoffs with Mexican-American manager Rick Renteria. It was the first time the White Sox qualified for the postseason since 2008, when another Latino manager, Ozzie Guillen, led the team to the playoffs.

Renteria's connection with Latino players had been part of the organization's plan for success for several years. His ability to communicate effectively, whether in English or Spanish, and also his familiarity with American and Latino cultures were components that the Sox hoped would enable Renteria to build clubhouse chemistry and success on the field. In a 2018 interview Renteria shared with me his approach to working with players.

"You have people coming from every walk of life. I don't try to target so much on where they're from. I look for baseball players. I look for guys that play the game … It's not in and of itself that you speak the language, Spanish or English or whatever language you speak … it has more to do with how you create a message, how you can present it. Make guys understand the concept that you're trying to impart to them. And if it works, they get it. And if it doesn't, you keep trying to find a new way."

Renteria kept trying to find a way. In 2020 he enjoyed his most successful season as a big league manager. He guided the White Sox to a 35-25 record and a second place finish in the AL Central.

Chicago's Latino Flavor is a Negro League Throwback

The Latino flavor of the White Sox 2020 squad was hard to miss. In no game was this more obvious than the August 1 contest versus the Royals. Cubans Luis Robert, Yoán Moncada, Abreu and Yasmani Grandal were penciled into the top of Chicago's batting order. It was the first time in MLB history Cuban-born players batted in the first four slots in a team's lineup. Ironically this historical moment occurred in Kansas City, where a hundred years earlier the Negro National League was founded by Rube Foster, an African-American ballplayer-turned-team owner who called Chicago home.

The 2020 White Sox provided powerful reminders of the history that Chicago shared with Black baseball. The Southsiders' former home ballpark, the original Comiskey Park, hosted Black baseball's showcase East-West Classic from the 1930s through the 1950s. The lineup Renteria put together throughout the 2020 campaign evoked memories of Negro League baseball. Even more, the Sox starting nine often resembled the lineups that the New York Cubans would have in the Negro Leagues.

Before he became "Minnie" and a star with the White Sox, Orestes Miñoso got his professional start in the U.S. with the NY Cubans club in 1946. The Negro League's Cubans team included Latino talent from the Dominican Republic, Puerto Rico, and Venezuela in addition to players from Cuba.

The 2020 Sox likewise featured its own regular cast of Latino players. Cuban native Grandal started most games behind the plate. Fellow Cuban Abreu anchored the infield at first. Nick Madrigal, a Mexican-American player from California, took regular turns at second base after his in-season promotion. The Sox lone African-American starter Tim Anderson continued to flourish at shortstop. A third Cuban, Moncada, fielded the hot corner.

Three Latinos composed the Sox starting outfield most games. Rookie Luis Robert patrolled center field. The manner Robert roamed the outfield at times seemed a modern version of Philadelphia Phillies center fielder Gary Maddox—of whom announcer Ralph Kiner once described "two-thirds of the earth is covered by water. The other third is covered by Gary Maddox." On occasion it verged on the comical. That much was clear when Robert called off Eloy Jiménez on a fly ball hit almost directly to the Sox left fielder. Jiménez struck a pose in faux anger and then laughed with his outfield partner. For Jiménez, 2020 saw his development into an offensive threat and not a sophomore slump. The same could not be said for fellow Venezuelan Nomar Mazara who took regular turns starting in right field although not quite getting on track at the plate.

The Sox moundsmen also featured a Latino contingent. The Latino relief corps enjoyed more success than their Latino counterpart in the starting rotation as Cuban-American Carlos Rodón was lost for much of 2020 due to injury and Dominican Reynaldo López started on the mound while battling his own injury woes and ineffectiveness. Alex Colomé and Jimmy Cordero were among the more called upon members of the Sox bullpen by Renteria, with Colomé often dominating in the closer role.

A Return to Postseason in Abnormal Times
As the White Sox positioned themselves to ascend the AL Central with their young nucleus of stars, the signing of Dallas Keuchel and Grandal as free agents proved important additions in 2020. Keuchel stabilized the Sox starting rotation, providing a veteran presence and an experienced postseason arm among Chicago's young starters. Grandal gave the team a catcher who could both command the game from behind the plate and pose a serious threat when he stepped into the batter's box.

Given the effects of the pandemic, the work of Renteria and other managers was more difficult than ever. Managing motivation, rule changes and the simple routine-building that goes into the marathon, or in this case the 5K, was a monumental task amidst postponements and positive test results. The feel at the ballpark was quite different. No fans were permitted to attend games until the World Series in October. The sounds of the game were amplified. No longer was the crack of the bat the sole sound that regularly reverberated throughout the ballparks. It was much easier to hear players bench jockeying, protesting umpires' calls, or encouraging one another. One could also hear Spanish more easily, whether it was the sounds of Bad Bunny or J Balvin as the walk-up music as batters strode to the plate or Latino players chatting each other up. This was particularly true of White Sox games.

In these abnormal times the White Sox qualified for an expanded postseason. For a while the Southsiders seemed they might even claim the AL Central title. Abreu stayed hot for almost the entire 60-game schedule, averaging an RBI a game and leading the AL in home runs and RBI while coming in fourth in batting average. Anderson expressed his joy of playing baseball while also speaking powerfully on racial issues inside and outside of baseball in the ongoing Black Lives Matter protests.

The Sox stumbled in late September, winning just two of their last ten games. The spiral allowed the Minnesota Twins to pass them in the Central standings and the home field advantage that would have come in the early rounds. The formula for success still seemed to be working as the Sox headed into Game 3 of the ALDS. Chicago hit Oakland starter Mike Fiers hard, though Robert's 487-foot home run ended up providing the lone run. Renteria gave the starting nod to rookie Dane Dunning but turned to the bullpen after just four batters. The relief corps fared poorly; they walked nine batters and ultimately lost the game. In the fallout, the front office sent Dunning and a prospect to the Texas Rangers for veteran Lance Lynn, hopeful they had landed someone to fill the role of a Game 3 postseason starter, and confident that, as the roster matures, they'll need another one.

Looking Back to Move Ahead

Renteria and the Sox parted ways after the Los Angeles Dodgers claimed their first World Series since 1988. The dismissal, described as a mutual decision, acknowledged that his "fingerprints will be all over that club and a big part of that success will be due to him" but that the choice was made "to take that next step ... putting us in a place to succeed." What elements Reneteria lacked for this next step went unstated. The Sox's managerial hire was itself a harkening back to the 1980s. The return of Tony LaRussa to the Southside surprised many. After all, LaRussa had been fired as White Sox manager 35 years ago—only three members of the 2020 squad were even alive then.

Hiring LaRussa is an abrupt departure from the plan that had paired Renteria with a young, Latino-centric squad. The move raised its own set of serious questions. How will the Latino players respond to LaRussa's managerial approach, communication style and ideas of managing personalities? Will Jimenéz and Robert flourish or flounder under LaRussa? The two budding Latino stars weren't even teenagers when LaRussa last managed.

It's a very real concern given his 2016 statements (which he doubled down on in early 2020) about players dishonoring the flag and his questioning the sincerity of Colin Kaepernick and other athletes engaging in peaceful protests, ideas that are out of step with the modern sports world with Black athletes and others openly expressing views in support of Black Lives Matter. His new shortstop, Tim Anderson, is at the forefront of these conversations. LaRussa took time during his first press conference to address his 2016 statements, which were made when he was in charge of the Arizona Diamondbacks' front office and responsible for setting an organizational tone. He said he was educated by what transpired in 2020. Yet, it is worth noting how interactions with players are quite different as a manager compared to the front office head. They are more personal, intimate and occur every day. White Sox success next season may well depend on how much their players trust LaRussa's evolution and the degree to which they feel he has their back in the game and that this support extends to their engagement with the public on social issues and on how their lives matter.

-Adrian Burgos, Jr. is a Professor of History at the University of Illinois.

Part 2: Player Analysis

Chicago White Sox 2021

PLAYER COMMENTS WITH GRAPHS

José Abreu 1B
Born: 01/29/87   Age: 34   Bats: R   Throws: R
Height: 6'3"   Weight: 250   Origin: International Free Agent, 2013

YEAR	TEAM	LVL	AGE	PA	R	2B	3B	HR	RBI	BB	K	SB	CS	AVG/OBP/SLG
2018	CHW	MLB	31	553	68	36	1	22	78	37	109	2	0	.265/.325/.473
2019	CHW	MLB	32	693	85	38	1	33	123	36	151	2	2	.284/.330/.503
2020	CHW	MLB	33	262	43	15	0	19	60	18	59	0	0	.317/.370/.617
2021 FS	CHW	MLB	34	600	84	29	1	29	95	38	141	2	1	.267/.330/.488
2021 DC	CHW	MLB	34	619	87	30	1	30	98	39	145	2	1	.267/.330/.488

Comparables: Cecil Fielder, Adrián González, Lee May

It's time to face facts that are borne out by the statistical record. After every veteran player with any latent trade value was dealt away from the White Sox over the course of the 2017 season, Abreu pulled a book from a bookshelf (let's say it was "Sense and Sensibility") in the White Sox clubhouse, opening up the hatch to a secret lair below Guaranteed Rate Field. After descending a staircase into the lair, Abreu entered a hyperbaric chamber. Within the chamber, he entered a sensory deprivation tank. Within the deprivation tank, he was encased in mylar so that he was preserved in mint condition, but with slits cut for ventilation so he did not die. Within the mylar, he was paired with a big ol' fuzzy grizzly bear who was also hibernating at the same time and served as his snuggle buddy for the duration of the 2018 and 2019 seasons. When he emerged in the middle of 2020 as play resumed, the 33-year-old Abreu was physically ready to mash like the days of old. As a parting gift for the doppelgänger who played in his stead for two seasons, Abreu offered him a lovely 1983 Bordeaux, as the secret lair doubles as a wine cellar. The doppelgänger was an above-average hitter in his own right and deserves a big league contract, though maybe he'll just come back and play for the White Sox next season.

YEAR	TEAM	LVL	AGE	PA	DRC+	BABIP	BRR	FRAA	WARP
2018	CHW	MLB	31	553	114	.294	0.0	1B(114): 4.9	2.3
2019	CHW	MLB	32	693	108	.320	-5.1	1B(125): -10.5	0.2
2020	CHW	MLB	33	262	140	.350	-0.4	1B(54): 2.7	2.0
2021 FS	CHW	MLB	34	600	120	.310	-0.8	1B -1	2.3
2021 DC	CHW	MLB	34	619	120	.310	-0.8	1B -1	2.4

José Abreu, continued

Batted Ball Distribution

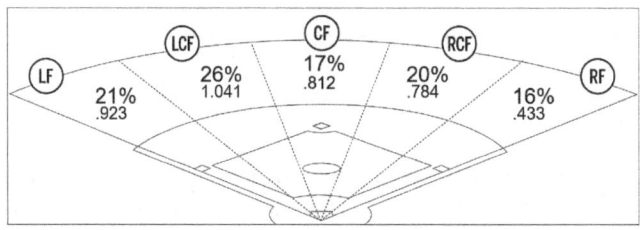

Strike Zone vs LHP   **Strike Zone vs RHP**

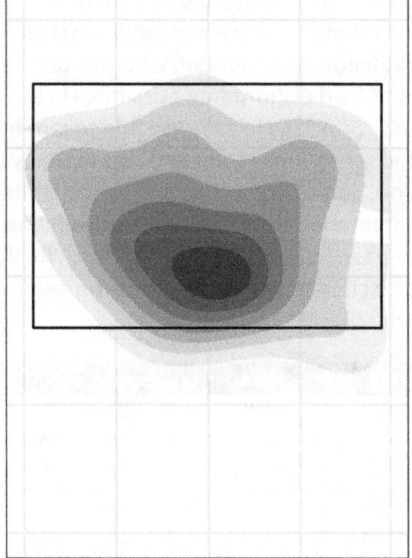

Tim Anderson SS

Born: 06/23/93   Age: 28   Bats: R   Throws: R
Height: 6'1"   Weight: 185   Origin: Round 1, 2013 Draft (#17 overall)

YEAR	TEAM	LVL	AGE	PA	R	2B	3B	HR	RBI	BB	K	SB	CS	AVG/OBP/SLG
2018	CHW	MLB	25	606	77	28	3	20	64	30	149	26	8	.240/.281/.406
2019	CHW	MLB	26	518	81	32	0	18	56	15	109	17	5	.335/.357/.508
2020	CHW	MLB	27	221	45	11	1	10	21	10	50	5	2	.322/.357/.529
2021 FS	CHW	MLB	28	600	78	27	2	21	66	24	152	15	5	.271/.306/.438
2021 DC	CHW	MLB	28	616	80	28	2	21	68	24	156	16	5	.271/.306/.438

Comparables: Dale Sveum, Ian Desmond, Kurt Abbott

It's of the deepest irony that the bat-flipping iconoclast who declares the game of baseball boring, outwardly expresses his lack of reverence for the sport's outmoded customs, and surely has inspired a legion of detractors, is perhaps the most old-school hitter in the league. Anderson has enough bat speed to turn and burn 20 home runs per season, and has in the past. But his breakout into a productive hitter largely lies in his predilection for so-called "good pieces of hitting." Every old crank who wishes they never had to hear about exit velocity, launch angle, or watch games determined by a couple of solo shots interspersed between dozens of strikeouts has the strangest bedfellow in Anderson, who has dedicated himself to flipping as many singles to right field as humanly possible. He lets everything on the outer half get deep and sprays it. He's impossible to jam because he can tuck his hands in quickly and rarely looks to pull. If you actually do get him to roll over a ball to the left side, he's a threat to sprint out an infield single. His exit velocity is unremarkable. His BABIP is unsustainably sky high. He also has a .331 batting average over his last 706 at-bats. Which leads to one last bit of irony: For those who cling to the value of batting average, posting .331 is the way to make it valuable.

YEAR	TEAM	LVL	AGE	PA	DRC+	BABIP	BRR	FRAA	WARP
2018	CHW	MLB	25	606	91	.289	6.5	SS(151): 9.1	3.8
2019	CHW	MLB	26	518	112	.399	4.3	SS(122): 1.7	3.9
2020	CHW	MLB	27	221	104	.383	1.7	SS(49): -1.3	0.8
2021 FS	CHW	MLB	28	600	100	.336	0.9	SS 1	2.0
2021 DC	CHW	MLB	28	616	100	.336	1.0	SS 1	2.1

Tim Anderson, continued

Batted Ball Distribution

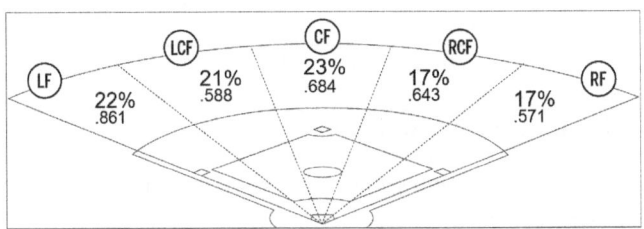

Strike Zone vs LHP   **Strike Zone vs RHP**

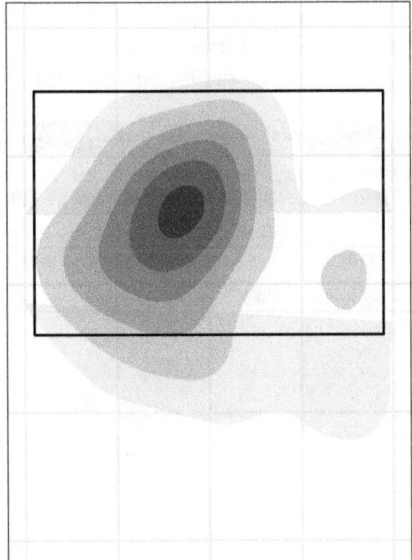

Chicago White Sox 2021

Adam Eaton RF

Born: 12/06/88   Age: 32   Bats: L   Throws: L
Height: 5'9"   Weight: 176   Origin: Round 19, 2010 Draft (#571 overall)

YEAR	TEAM	LVL	AGE	PA	R	2B	3B	HR	RBI	BB	K	SB	CS	AVG/OBP/SLG
2018	WAS	MLB	29	370	55	18	1	5	33	38	64	9	1	.301/.394/.411
2019	WAS	MLB	30	656	103	25	7	15	49	65	106	15	3	.279/.365/.428
2020	WAS	MLB	31	176	22	11	1	4	17	12	32	3	0	.226/.285/.384
2021 FS	CHW	MLB	32	600	74	24	3	12	61	56	120	11	4	.252/.336/.384
2021 DC	CHW	MLB	32	567	70	23	3	12	57	53	114	11	4	.252/.336/.384

Comparables: Lloyd Moseby, Tony Gonzalez, Mitch Webster

A mortgage is something that you're initially excited about—a house! A new and shiny house! Then the first major renovation hits, then you're like—a house! A terrible and costly house! Then it mostly settles into being something that will never be as valuable as it used to be, even though you have to keep paying for it for longer than you'd like. The whole experience makes you really pine for that old apartment you had before signing the mortgage, especially when that old apartment is Lucas Giolito and that house is post-prime Adam Eaton, who the Nationals elected against keeping around despite a track record of being an above-average hitter. Eaton rejoined the White Sox on a one-year deal, suggesting they did indeed pine for that old apartment.

YEAR	TEAM	LVL	AGE	PA	DRC+	BABIP	BRR	FRAA	WARP
2018	WAS	MLB	29	370	106	.364	0.4	RF(67): 5.7, LF(10): -0.5	1.7
2019	WAS	MLB	30	656	101	.319	3.6	RF(139): 4.3, LF(7): -0.0	2.5
2020	WAS	MLB	31	176	90	.260	1.1	RF(41): 0.2	0.2
2021 FS	CHW	MLB	32	600	100	.302	0.5	RF 3, LF 0	1.7
2021 DC	CHW	MLB	32	567	100	.302	0.5	RF 3	1.6

Adam Eaton, continued

Batted Ball Distribution

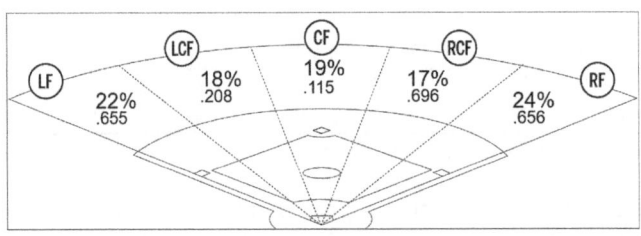

Strike Zone vs LHP **Strike Zone vs RHP**

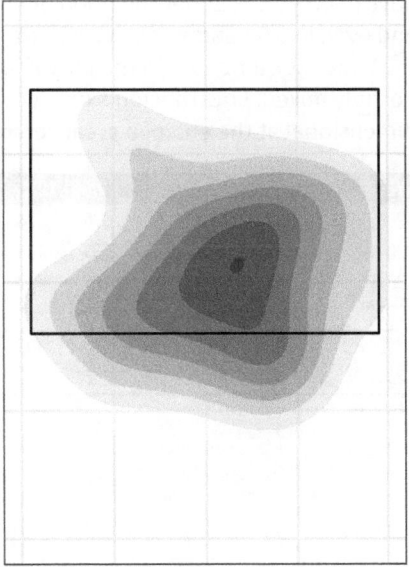

Edwin Encarnación 1B

Born: 01/07/83   Age: 38   Bats: R   Throws: R
Height: 6'1"   Weight: 230   Origin: Round 9, 2000 Draft (#274 overall)

YEAR	TEAM	LVL	AGE	PA	R	2B	3B	HR	RBI	BB	K	SB	CS	AVG/OBP/SLG
2018	CLE	MLB	35	579	74	16	1	32	107	63	132	3	0	.246/.336/.474
2019	SEA	MLB	36	289	48	7	0	21	49	41	55	0	1	.241/.356/.531
2019	NYY	MLB	36	197	33	11	0	13	37	17	48	0	0	.249/.325/.531
2020	CHW	MLB	37	181	19	5	0	10	19	16	54	0	0	.157/.250/.377
2021 FS	CHW	MLB	38	600	75	20	0	29	82	68	165	1	1	.216/.318/.426
2021 DC	CHW	MLB	38	350	43	12	0	17	48	40	96	0	1	.216/.318/.426

Comparables: Paul Konerko, Kevin Millar, Tino Martinez

While there are some enormous cockatoos that can live up to 80 years, the sort of smaller parrot you might let perch on your forearm as you circle the bases typically has a shelf life of 15-20 trips around the sun. Signs that your parrot might be nearing the end of its impressive run would be an exploding infield pop-up rate, pronounced troubles turning around velocity, and of course, "parrot fever." Encarnación didn't experience that last one in 2020, but there have been noises under the hood of his batted ball profile for a few years now, and even in a 60-game season, the engine just began to spurt smoke by the time the White Sox limped into the playoffs. And unlike how this metaphor became horribly mixed, Encarnación's production has become frustratingly one-dimensional at the end of a great career.

YEAR	TEAM	LVL	AGE	PA	DRC+	BABIP	BRR	FRAA	WARP
2018	CLE	MLB	35	579	124	.265	-5.1	1B(23): 0.8	2.1
2019	SEA	MLB	36	289	134	.220	0.6	1B(45): -0.6, 2B(1): -0.0	1.7
2019	NYY	MLB	36	197	127	.267	-1.7	1B(12): -0.4	0.8
2020	CHW	MLB	37	181	92	.156	-0.7		0.1
2021 FS	CHW	MLB	38	600	103	.257	-0.9	1B -2, 2B 0	0.8
2021 DC	CHW	MLB	38	350	103	.257	-0.5	1B -1, 2B 0	0.5

Edwin Encarnación, continued

Batted Ball Distribution

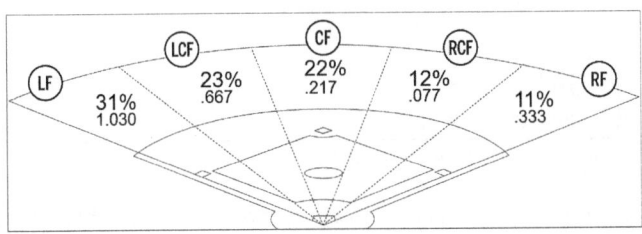

Strike Zone vs LHP   ### Strike Zone vs RHP

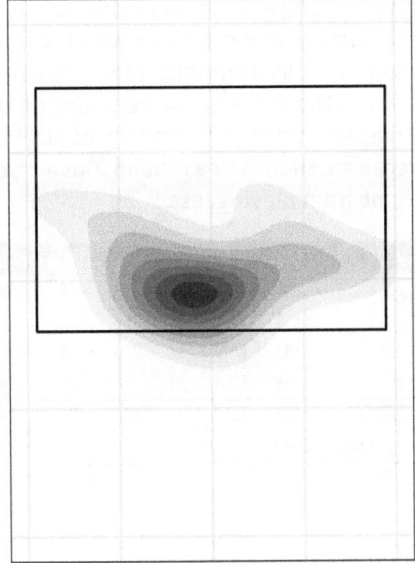

Adam Engel CF

Born: 12/09/91   Age: 29   Bats: R   Throws: R
Height: 6'2"   Weight: 220   Origin: Round 19, 2013 Draft (#573 overall)

YEAR	TEAM	LVL	AGE	PA	R	2B	3B	HR	RBI	BB	K	SB	CS	AVG/OBP/SLG
2018	CHW	MLB	26	463	49	17	4	6	29	18	129	16	8	.235/.279/.336
2019	CHA	AAA	27	277	43	13	4	9	29	22	62	13	3	.270/.347/.464
2019	CHW	MLB	27	248	26	10	2	6	26	14	78	3	3	.242/.304/.383
2020	CHW	MLB	28	93	11	5	1	3	12	3	19	1	0	.295/.333/.477
2021 FS	CHW	MLB	29	600	66	24	4	15	62	39	175	17	7	.221/.287/.367
2021 DC	CHW	MLB	29	245	27	9	1	6	25	16	71	7	3	.221/.287/.367

Comparables: Reggie Taylor, Kimera Bartee, Jordan Schafer

Years of howling "Adam Engel is a backup at best" from the bleachers and into the swirling winds of Guaranteed Rate Field was finally intoned in 2020, after three years of muscular outfield defense and very musclebound swings-and-misses at the plate. After years of struggles, it can be forgiven that the message was garbled into "Adam Engel is a backup, the best." Sure, this turn of phrase is as corny as buying into Engel's 93 plate appearances in 2020 as proof that he's awesome now. But his effectiveness against left-handed pitching has proven fairly sticky, and combines with his typically sterling and fleet-footed defense. That's usually a starter set for, yes, a decent backup outfielder. First called up in 2017 as the White Sox were selling off every major league asset of consequence, Engel was thrust into a bunch of playing time he would have otherwise never received, thanks to a rebuild. But a stable role and production might finally come from playing less.

YEAR	TEAM	LVL	AGE	PA	DRC+	BABIP	BRR	FRAA	WARP
2018	CHW	MLB	26	463	68	.322	1.5	CF(140): 10.0	1.0
2019	CHA	AAA	27	277	92	.328	4.0	CF(58): 7.4, LF(5): -0.4, RF(1): -0.1	1.6
2019	CHW	MLB	27	248	64	.343	0.6	CF(86): 0.8	-0.1
2020	CHW	MLB	28	93	85	.348	0.2	RF(25): -0.6, LF(9): -0.6, CF(3): -0.6	-0.1
2021 FS	CHW	MLB	29	600	79	.295	1.7	CF 2, RF -1	0.1
2021 DC	CHW	MLB	29	245	79	.295	0.7	CF 1, RF 0	-0.1

Adam Engel, continued

Batted Ball Distribution

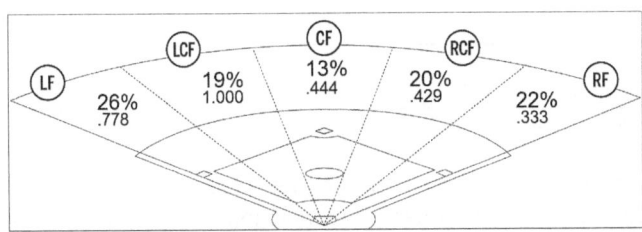

Strike Zone vs LHP   Strike Zone vs RHP

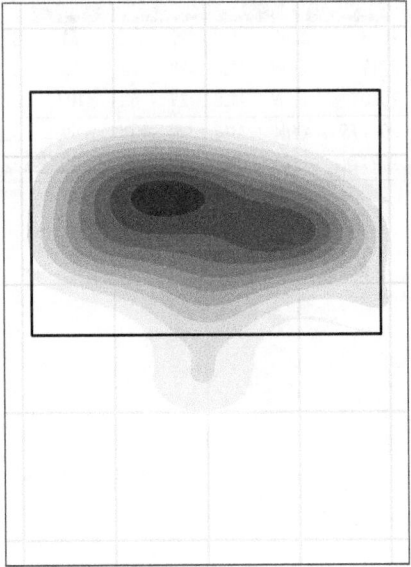

Leury García CF

Born: 03/18/91 Age: 30 Bats: S Throws: R
Height: 5'8" Weight: 185 Origin: International Free Agent, 2007

YEAR	TEAM	LVL	AGE	PA	R	2B	3B	HR	RBI	BB	K	SB	CS	AVG/OBP/SLG
2018	CHW	MLB	27	275	23	7	4	4	32	9	69	12	1	.271/.303/.376
2019	CHW	MLB	28	618	93	27	3	8	40	21	139	15	5	.279/.310/.378
2020	CHW	MLB	29	63	6	1	0	3	8	4	9	0	0	.271/.317/.441
2021 FS	CHW	MLB	30	600	70	24	2	13	59	30	140	14	6	.260/.307/.385
2021 DC	CHW	MLB	30	202	23	8	0	4	20	10	47	4	2	.260/.307/.385

Comparables: Randy Kutcher, John Shelby, Juan Lagares

If there's some level of utilitymanitude that is too perfect for this world, surely García has found it. How else does someone banjax two separate seasons with injuries related to sliding head first into first base? The White Sox have lauded García's ability to "roll out of bed and play," but such boasts were undermined by his actual attempt to do just that in the 2020 Wild Card Series, fresh off a seven-week absence for a torn left thumb ligament.

YEAR	TEAM	LVL	AGE	PA	DRC+	BABIP	BRR	FRAA	WARP
2018	CHW	MLB	27	275	74	.355	1.8	LF(40): 1.4, CF(26): -0.8, RF(16): 0.7	0.3
2019	CHW	MLB	28	618	78	.353	7.9	CF(80): -5.4, RF(45): -2.7, LF(24): -0.3	0.3
2020	CHW	MLB	29	63	107	.277	0.2	SS(10): 0.3, 2B(5): 0.0, RF(3): -0.0	0.3
2021 FS	CHW	MLB	30	600	89	.325	0.9	SS 0, 2B 1	1.1
2021 DC	CHW	MLB	30	202	89	.325	0.3	SS 0, 2B 0	0.4

Leury García, continued

Batted Ball Distribution

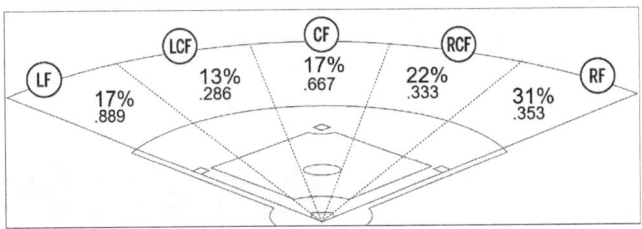

Strike Zone vs LHP

Strike Zone vs RHP

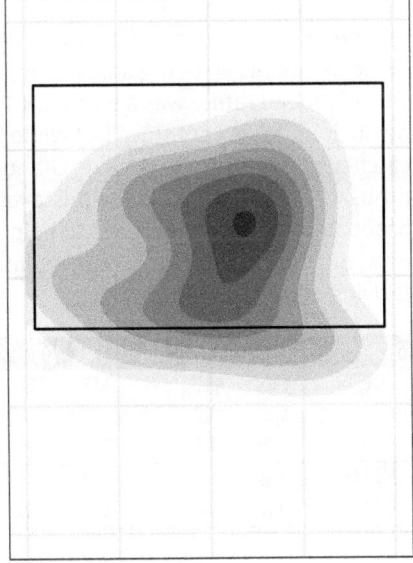

Yasmani Grandal C

Born: 11/08/88   Age: 32   Bats: S   Throws: R
Height: 6'2"   Weight: 230   Origin: Round 1, 2010 Draft (#12 overall)

YEAR	TEAM	LVL	AGE	PA	R	2B	3B	HR	RBI	BB	K	SB	CS	AVG/OBP/SLG
2018	LAD	MLB	29	518	65	23	2	24	68	72	124	2	1	.241/.349/.466
2019	MIL	MLB	30	632	79	26	2	28	77	109	139	5	1	.246/.380/.468
2020	CHW	MLB	31	194	27	7	0	8	27	30	58	0	0	.230/.351/.422
2021 FS	CHW	MLB	32	600	82	21	1	25	75	88	174	3	2	.220/.340/.417
2021 DC	CHW	MLB	32	551	75	20	1	23	69	80	159	2	2	.220/.340/.417

Comparables: Jorge Posada, Mickey Tettleton, Geovany Soto

Not allowed to review in-game video of his swings due to a combination of COVID-19 and anti-Astros restrictions, Grandal's mistake-speed power bat racked up a career-high strikeout rate in 2020. Rightly assessing that pitch-framing is valued above all, Grandal also racked up his normally large number of wild pitches and strangely dropped tags. On an Instagram post dedicated to his wedding anniversary with his wife, a commenter asked him why his speed rating was a 6 on MLB The Show. It seems like the answer should be obvious: He is very slow. But while you may not like it, this is what peak catcher performance looks like. Grandal batflips his many walks, has cool bat drops when he uppercuts the mistakes he runs into and games the goofy system baseball has for calling strikes to help out his pitcher. Aesthetically, it's not the best. But Grandal knows how the game is being played, and for now, is still thriving at it.

YEAR	TEAM	P. COUNT	FRM RUNS	BLK RUNS	THRW RUNS	TOT RUNS
2018	LAD	16816	15.7	0.8	0.1	16.5
2019	MIL	18740	19.4	1.8	-0.1	21.1
2020	CHW	4830	3.7	0.3	-0.2	3.8
2021	CHW	14430	16.7	-0.6	1.0	17.1
2021	CHW	14430	16.7	0.4	1.0	18.0

YEAR	TEAM	LVL	AGE	PA	DRC+	BABIP	BRR	FRAA	WARP
2018	LAD	MLB	29	518	112	.278	-4.4	C(135): 17.7, 1B(2): -0.0	4.7
2019	MIL	MLB	30	632	123	.279	-7.5	C(137): 19.9, 1B(20): 0.2	6.1
2020	CHW	MLB	31	194	108	.299	0.1	C(32): 1.0, 1B(6): -0.1	1.2
2021 FS	CHW	MLB	32	600	108	.282	-0.6	C 14, 1B 0	4.3
2021 DC	CHW	MLB	32	551	108	.282	-0.6	C 17, 1B 0	4.2

Yasmani Grandal, continued

Batted Ball Distribution

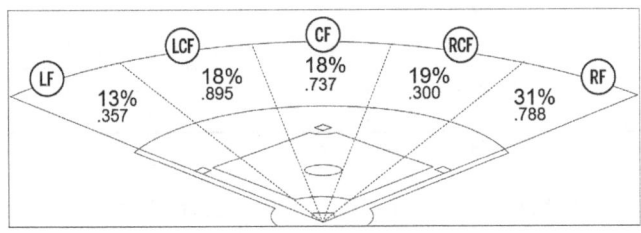

Strike Zone vs LHP   Strike Zone vs RHP

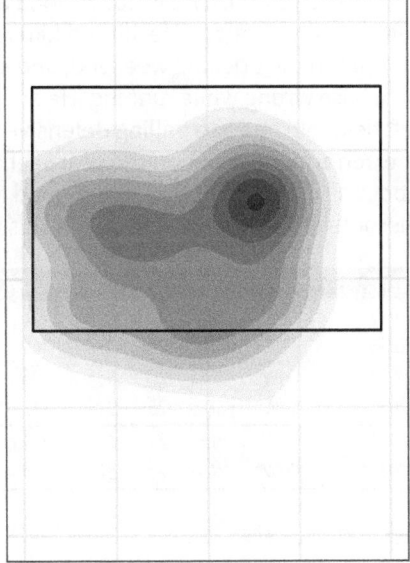

Eloy Jiménez LF

Born: 11/27/96 Age: 24 Bats: R Throws: R
Height: 6'4" Weight: 235 Origin: International Free Agent, 2013

YEAR	TEAM	LVL	AGE	PA	R	2B	3B	HR	RBI	BB	K	SB	CS	AVG/OBP/SLG
2018	BIR	AA	21	228	36	15	2	10	42	18	39	0	0	.317/.368/.556
2018	CHA	AAA	21	228	28	13	1	12	33	14	30	0	1	.355/.399/.597
2019	CHW	MLB	22	504	69	18	2	31	79	30	134	0	0	.267/.315/.513
2020	CHW	MLB	23	226	26	14	0	14	41	12	56	0	0	.296/.332/.559
2021 FS	CHW	MLB	24	600	82	28	2	35	95	37	155	0	1	.274/.324/.521
2021 DC	CHW	MLB	24	570	78	27	1	33	90	35	147	0	1	.274/.324/.521

Comparables: Pete Incaviglia, Justin Upton, Greg Luzinski

Humanity is capable of containing multitudes, reconciling contradictions within itself, and living as a dichotomy. As such, Jiménez is a pure, almost poetic savant at the plate. He's almost too good at hitting to care about pitch selection. His ceaseless aggression is counterbalanced by the larger discipline of his overall goals; a steadfast refusal to give in to the trap of pulling, knowing he's too strong to concede to a search for power. He swings at anything, yet tightens up in key situations. He is not as good as he will be yet. He is also, almost self-referentially, a galoot. He injured himself banging his head against the fence on defense in the opening weekend, and effectively ended his season by stepping on a base wrong while running. He flopped into the protective netting along the left field foul line as a galling defensive lowlight in August, and then repeated the performance later on the year seemingly as a bit. He is both self-aware about his fielding shortcomings, good humored about it, and burning with discontent about it. He can do it all, as we all can.

YEAR	TEAM	LVL	AGE	PA	DRC+	BABIP	BRR	FRAA	WARP
2018	BIR	AA	21	228	158	.344	-1.3	LF(30): -3.6, RF(13): -1.8	0.7
2018	CHA	AAA	21	228	169	.371	-1.8	LF(41): -0.2, RF(6): 0.0	1.8
2019	CHW	MLB	22	504	105	.308	1.0	LF(114): -0.7	1.7
2020	CHW	MLB	23	226	113	.340	-0.4	LF(54): -7.9	0.1
2021 FS	CHW	MLB	24	600	124	.321	-0.8	LF -1, RF 0	3.3
2021 DC	CHW	MLB	24	570	124	.321	-0.7	LF -1	3.1

Eloy Jiménez, continued

Batted Ball Distribution

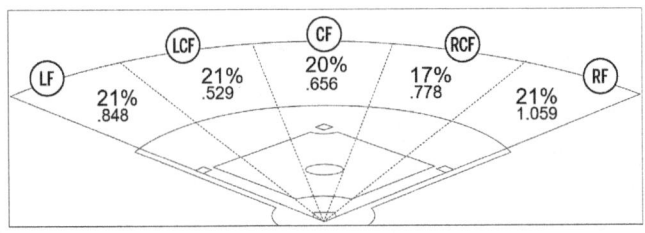

Strike Zone vs LHP   **Strike Zone vs RHP**

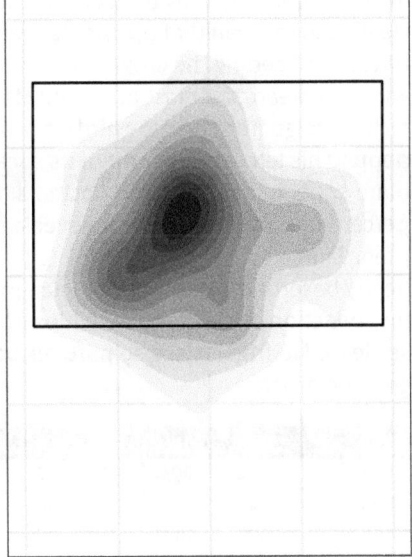

Nick Madrigal 2B

Born: 03/05/97   Age: 24   Bats: R   Throws: R
Height: 5'8"   Weight: 175   Origin: Round 1, 2018 Draft (#4 overall)

YEAR	TEAM	LVL	AGE	PA	R	2B	3B	HR	RBI	BB	K	SB	CS	AVG/OBP/SLG
2018	WSX	ROK	21	17	2	0	0	0	1	1	0	0	1	.154/.353/.154
2018	KAN	LO-A	21	49	9	3	0	0	6	1	0	2	2	.341/.347/.409
2018	WS	HI-A	21	107	14	4	0	0	9	5	5	6	3	.306/.355/.347
2019	WS	HI-A	22	218	20	10	2	2	27	17	6	17	4	.272/.346/.377
2019	BIR	AA	22	180	30	11	2	1	16	14	5	14	6	.341/.400/.451
2019	CHA	AAA	22	134	26	6	1	1	12	13	5	4	3	.331/.398/.424
2020	CHW	MLB	23	109	8	3	0	0	11	4	7	2	1	.340/.376/.369
2021 FS	CHW	MLB	24	600	72	32	2	8	64	35	50	19	8	.295/.349/.408
2021 DC	CHW	MLB	24	492	59	26	1	7	52	29	41	15	7	.295/.349/.408

Comparables: Breyvic Valera, Jarrett Hoffpauir, Eric Sogard

Madrigal's bold and ceaseless pursuit of on-brand activities has reached the point where it's necessary to arrange them in a hierarchy. His 3.3 percent swinging strike rate is low, but two players with 100 plate appearances posted lower figures, and they both chased out of the zone less often than Madrigal. He'll need to clean that up. Similarly, his 6.4 percent strikeout rate was second-lowest, but ceding the crown to Tommy La Stella will probably stick with him all winter. Instead, the most on-brand Madrigal accomplishment of 2020 was trying so hard to go from first-to-third on a fairly firm single to center field that he popped his left shoulder out of its socket, limiting his debut season to just 109 plate appearances. (He also posted a higher on-base rate than slugging percentage, but that's a basic-level Madrigal feat). In future years, Chicago's preordained spark plug will look to substitute increased defensive precision and heady baserunning, rather than just merely hyper-aggressive baserunning, to his collection of on-brand activities. Until that comes together, we'll have to settle for Madrigal trying so hard his body breaks apart as proof that he's the genuine article.

YEAR	TEAM	LVL	AGE	PA	DRC+	BABIP	BRR	FRAA	WARP
2018	WSX	ROK	21	17		.154			
2018	KAN	LO-A	21	49	143	.319	1.1	2B(12): 0.9	0.5
2018	WS	HI-A	21	107	120	.319	0.0	2B(25): -1.8	0.1
2019	WS	HI-A	22	218	114	.269	3.6	2B(41): 3.4	1.6
2019	BIR	AA	22	180	154	.348	0.3	2B(39): 0.1	1.6
2019	CHA	AAA	22	134	102	.336	0.5	2B(28): 1.5	0.6
2020	CHW	MLB	23	109	101	.365	-1.5	2B(29): 1.7	0.4
2021 FS	CHW	MLB	24	600	110	.313	0.9	2B 1, SS 0	2.8
2021 DC	CHW	MLB	24	492	110	.313	0.8	2B 1	2.3

Nick Madrigal, continued

Batted Ball Distribution

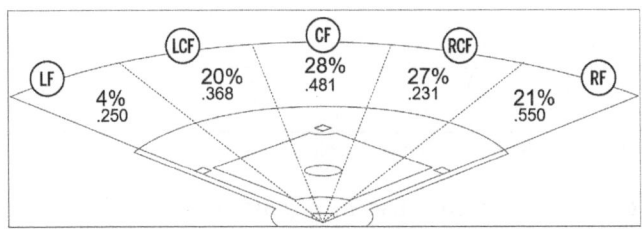

Strike Zone vs LHP   Strike Zone vs RHP

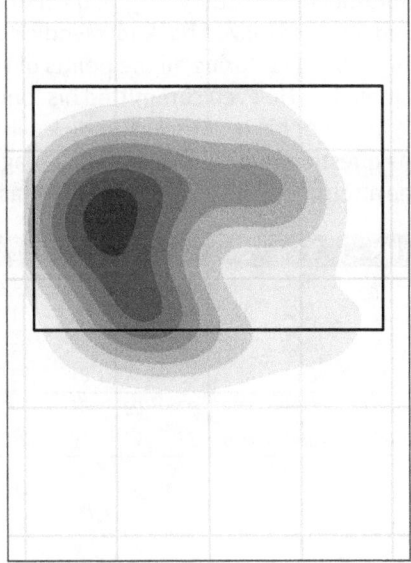

Danny Mendick SS

Born: 09/28/93   Age: 27   Bats: R   Throws: R
Height: 5'10"   Weight: 195   Origin: Round 22, 2015 Draft (#652 overall)

YEAR	TEAM	LVL	AGE	PA	R	2B	3B	HR	RBI	BB	K	SB	CS	AVG/OBP/SLG
2018	BIR	AA	24	529	62	25	0	14	59	57	90	20	10	.247/.340/.395
2019	CHA	AAA	25	558	75	26	1	17	64	66	96	19	8	.279/.368/.444
2019	CHW	MLB	25	40	6	0	0	2	4	1	11	0	0	.308/.325/.462
2020	CHW	MLB	26	114	11	4	1	3	6	6	25	0	1	.243/.281/.383
2021 FS	CHW	MLB	27	600	69	25	1	16	66	49	143	5	3	.235/.307/.380
2021 DC	CHW	MLB	27	191	22	8	0	5	21	15	45	1	1	.235/.307/.380

Comparables: Ramón Urías, Ian Kinsler, Corban Joseph

The truly great backup second basemen constantly escalate the tension of whether they should be a starting second baseman. An idealized representative would have to somehow perform as well as possible in their role, while never actually challenging the appropriateness of said role. To this end, Mendick hit .303/.338/.515 in a rollicking three-week period while White Sox starting second baseman Nick Madrigal was on the injured list. With Mendick's multi-positional utility, it gave birth to calls that he should be a starter of some kind. As an idealized backup, Mendick defused this hysteria by hitting .146/.186/.171 during all the points of the season where Madrigal was not on the injured list. He even committed his lone error of the season while Madrigal was healthy. For his next trick, Mendick will need to defuse the tension surrounding the question that he is not a major leaguer, since the White Sox optioned him to the alternate site by the end of the season.

YEAR	TEAM	LVL	AGE	PA	DRC+	BABIP	BRR	FRAA	WARP
2018	BIR	AA	24	529	109	.275	1.4	SS(131): -4.2	1.6
2019	CHA	AAA	25	558	102	.313	0.3	2B(48): 4.2, SS(42): 2.4, 3B(38): -0.9	2.8
2019	CHW	MLB	25	40	88	.385	0.0	SS(5): 0.0, 2B(3): -0.4, 3B(3): 0.7	0.1
2020	CHW	MLB	26	114	81	.287	0.2	2B(28): 2.9, SS(4): 0.0, 3B(3): 0.1	0.4
2021 FS	CHW	MLB	27	600	89	.290	-0.3	3B 1, 2B 2	1.2
2021 DC	CHW	MLB	27	191	89	.290	-0.1	3B 0, 2B 1	0.3

Danny Mendick, continued

Batted Ball Distribution

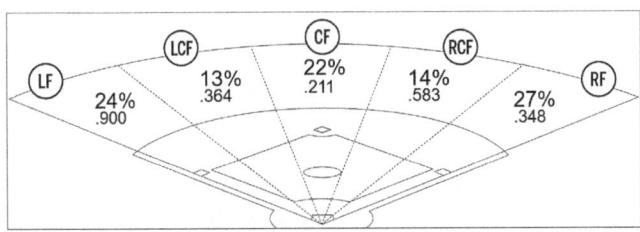

Strike Zone vs LHP

Strike Zone vs RHP

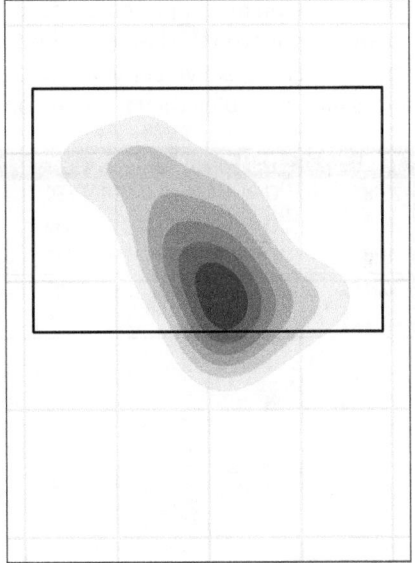

Yoán Moncada 3B

Born: 05/27/95   Age: 26   Bats: S   Throws: R
Height: 6'2"   Weight: 225   Origin: International Free Agent, 2015

YEAR	TEAM	LVL	AGE	PA	R	2B	3B	HR	RBI	BB	K	SB	CS	AVG/OBP/SLG
2018	CHW	MLB	23	650	73	32	6	17	61	67	217	12	6	.235/.315/.400
2019	CHW	MLB	24	559	83	34	5	25	79	40	154	10	3	.315/.367/.548
2020	CHW	MLB	25	231	28	8	3	6	24	28	72	0	0	.225/.320/.385
2021 FS	CHW	MLB	26	600	83	25	3	21	70	67	193	12	6	.243/.334/.426
2021 DC	CHW	MLB	26	605	83	25	3	21	71	67	195	13	6	.243/.334/.426

Comparables: Brandon Lowe, Danny Espinosa, Ryan McMahon

If the hundreds of thousands of deaths, millions of cases and more or less the shutdown of the global economy weren't enough to convince you that COVID-19 is a serious issue, perhaps the trials of a healthy 25-year-old Moncada will resonate. Statistically, he simply went back to normal after simple variance saw him cosplay as a top-50 position player in the sport for all of 2019. Physically, Moncada was a ghost after testing positive for the virus in July. After every burst of speed, reserved for only when the moment truly demanded it from him, his hands were planted squarely on his hips as he strained to regain his breath. When he squeezed the handle of his bat, the strength he always felt had eroded and his average exit velocity plummeted. He is young, he is in fabulous shape and is an incredible athlete, and no one knows what comes next.

YEAR	TEAM	LVL	AGE	PA	DRC+	BABIP	BRR	FRAA	WARP
2018	CHW	MLB	23	650	89	.344	-0.4	2B(149): -12.7	-0.2
2019	CHW	MLB	24	559	123	.406	3.5	3B(129): 10.3	5.1
2020	CHW	MLB	25	231	87	.315	0.8	3B(52): 1.5	0.3
2021 FS	CHW	MLB	26	600	107	.342	0.8	3B 2, 2B 0	2.3
2021 DC	CHW	MLB	26	605	107	.342	0.8	3B 2	2.0

Yoán Moncada, continued

Batted Ball Distribution

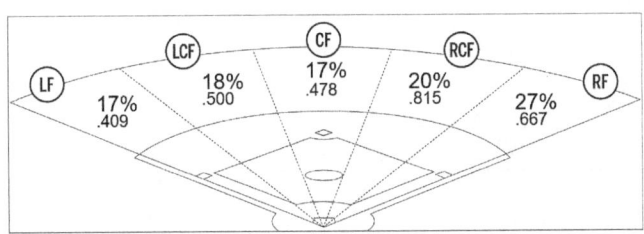

Strike Zone vs LHP   Strike Zone vs RHP

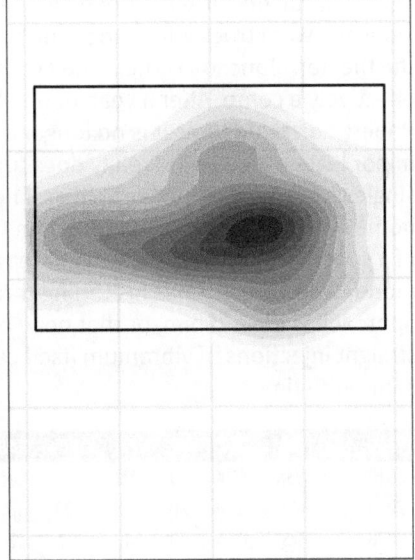

Luis Robert CF

Born: 08/03/97 Age: 23 Bats: R Throws: R
Height: 6'2" Weight: 210 Origin: International Free Agent, 2017

YEAR	TEAM	LVL	AGE	PA	R	2B	3B	HR	RBI	BB	K	SB	CS	AVG/OBP/SLG
2018	WSX	ROK	20	18	5	2	1	0	2	0	3	3	0	.389/.389/.611
2018	KAN	LO-A	20	50	5	3	1	0	4	4	12	4	2	.289/.360/.400
2018	WS	HI-A	20	140	21	6	1	0	11	8	37	8	2	.244/.317/.309
2019	WS	HI-A	21	84	21	5	3	8	24	4	20	8	2	.453/.512/.920
2019	BIR	AA	21	244	43	16	3	8	29	13	54	21	6	.314/.362/.518
2019	CHA	AAA	21	223	44	10	5	16	39	11	55	7	3	.297/.341/.634
2020	CHW	MLB	22	227	33	8	0	11	31	20	73	9	2	.233/.302/.436
2021 FS	CHW	MLB	23	600	74	23	3	25	79	40	196	19	6	.234/.298/.427
2021 DC	CHW	MLB	23	551	68	21	3	23	72	37	180	17	6	.234/.298/.427

Comparables: Victor Robles, Larry Hisle, Wily Mo Pena

In spring training of 2018, Yoán Moncada went to the movies. He saw the late Chadwick Boseman portray King T'Challa on screen, or mostly a CGI facsimile of him hopping onto speeding cars, and glowing purple at select intervals and whatever the hell else happened in that movie. In that profound moment, Moncada was struck with a thought: Luis Robert...or so the story goes. Out of the theater, Moncada came armed with a nickname for Robert—La Pantera—and effectively a comp. After a year, or one bizarrely shortened season, in the majors, Robert's dizzying toolset is no longer an international scouting tall tale or even a minor league legend. He really does turn every bouncer into a potential infield single, scoot around center field as if he were riding a moped, and swat massive home runs with apparent ease. But in this gritty, realistic workup of the premise of a superhero trying to play major league baseball, Robert's 2020 included the month where he just has his timing thrown off by pitchers changing their approaches toward him, or that none of the science in Wakanda nor even straight injections of vibranium itself can instill plate discipline. That can only come with time.

YEAR	TEAM	LVL	AGE	PA	DRC+	BABIP	BRR	FRAA	WARP
2018	WSX	ROK	20	18		.467			
2018	KAN	LO-A	20	50	104	.394	-0.2	CF(10): 0.0	0.0
2018	WS	HI-A	20	140	84	.341	0.5	CF(27): 3.1, RF(4): -0.4, LF(1): -0.1	0.2
2019	WS	HI-A	21	84	273	.553	-1.2	CF(13): 1.9	1.6
2019	BIR	AA	21	244	127	.384	2.5	CF(36): 1.9, RF(7): -0.8, LF(2): 0.0	1.8
2019	CHA	AAA	21	223	114	.324	1.2	CF(47): 6.5	1.7
2020	CHW	MLB	22	227	86	.300	0.1	CF(56): 11.2	1.4
2021 FS	CHW	MLB	23	600	95	.315	1.8	CF 9, LF 0	2.6
2021 DC	CHW	MLB	23	551	95	.315	1.7	CF 8	2.4

Luis Robert, continued

Batted Ball Distribution

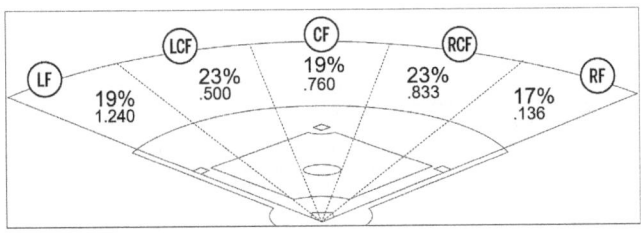

Strike Zone vs LHP   **Strike Zone vs RHP**

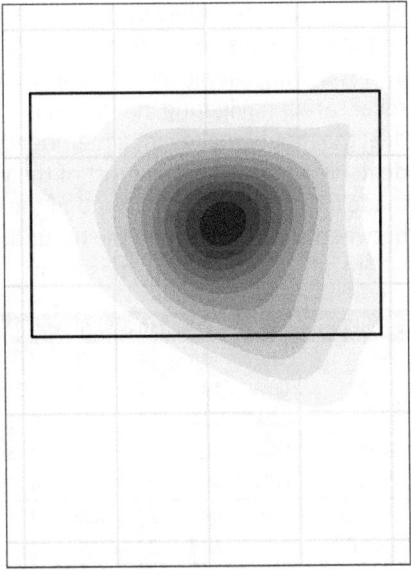

Aaron Bummer LHP

Born: 09/21/93   Age: 27   Bats: L   Throws: L
Height: 6'3"   Weight: 215   Origin: Round 19, 2014 Draft (#558 overall)

YEAR	TEAM	LVL	AGE	W	L	SV	G	GS	IP	H	HR	BB/9	K/9	K	GB%	BABIP
2018	CHA	AAA	24	2	3	0	31	0	30^2	27	0	3.2	8.8	30	63.2%	.314
2018	CHW	MLB	24	0	1	0	37	0	31^2	40	1	2.8	9.9	35	62.2%	.402
2019	CHA	AAA	25	0	0	0	5	0	7^2	7	0	2.3	7.0	6	87.0%	.333
2019	CHW	MLB	25	0	0	1	58	0	67^2	43	4	3.2	8.0	60	69.7%	.229
2020	CHW	MLB	26	1	0	0	9	0	9^1	5	0	4.8	13.5	14	68.4%	.263
2021 FS	CHW	MLB	27	2	2	3	57	0	50	43	4	4.6	10.0	55	63.1%	.297
2021 DC	CHW	MLB	27	2	2	3	52	0	56.3	48	5	4.6	10.0	62	63.1%	.297

Comparables: Keynan Middleton, A.J. Minter, Jonathan Holder

After his breakout 2019 campaign, Bummer was placed in an unexpected position: Kids were contacting him on social media trying to replicate his wonky mechanics. He quite simply had always thought his mechanics were a mess, and possibly a hindrance. Bummer's low three-quarters delivery conjures the word "sling" to mind as clearly as any major league throwing motion. His professional career had previously been defined by struggles, injury and command issues. Even stranger, he found himself spending the first part of the year weighing a long-term extension offer, after assuming he would spend his relief career navigating injury and performance flare-ups. In his first season on a deal that could make him a member of the White Sox through 2026, he indeed dealt with injury, missed most of the year with a bicep nerve issue and only made a tepid return by the end of the season in time for a brief playoff run. In between all this, when on the mound, he wielded that sling like David, which is where all the attention comes from.

YEAR	TEAM	LVL	AGE	WHIP	ERA	DRA-	WARP	MPH	FB%	WHF	CSP
2018	CHA	AAA	24	1.24	2.64	71	0.6				
2018	CHW	MLB	24	1.58	4.26	82	0.4	95.0	65.8%	24.0%	
2019	CHA	AAA	25	1.17	2.35	71	0.2				
2019	CHW	MLB	25	0.99	2.13	61	1.7	97.3	76.1%	24.4%	
2020	CHW	MLB	26	1.07	0.96	74	0.2	97.2	85.1%	35.0%	
2021 FS	CHW	MLB	27	1.38	3.71	87	0.6	96.8	75.5%	25.9%	49.9%
2021 DC	CHW	MLB	27	1.38	3.71	87	0.7	96.8	75.5%	25.9%	49.9%

Aaron Bummer, continued

Pitch Shape vs LHH

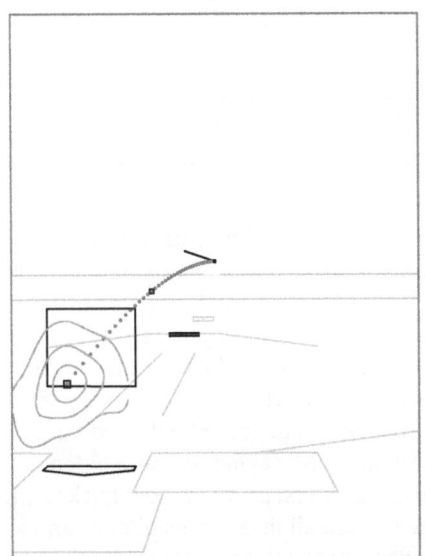

Pitch Shape vs RHH

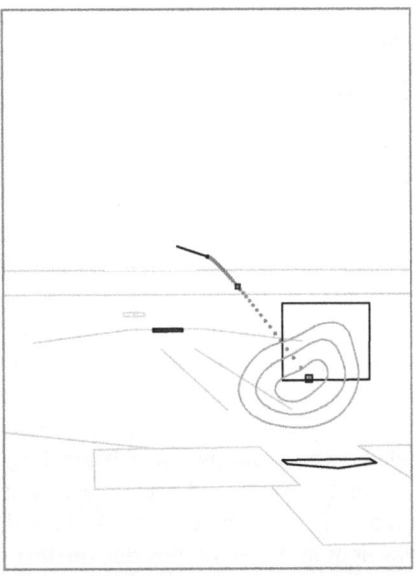

Type	Frequency	Velocity	H Movement	V Movement
☐ Sinker	84.4%	95.9 [118]	12.3 [106]	-25.3 [85]
+ Cutter	9.1%	88.9 [104]	-0.9 [94]	-29.7 [79]
▽ Slider	5.8%	83.9 [100]	-14.7 [136]	-40.1 [82]

Zack Burdi RHP

Born: 03/09/95   Age: 26   Bats: R   Throws: R
Height: 6'3"   Weight: 210   Origin: Round 1, 2016 Draft (#26 overall)

YEAR	TEAM	LVL	AGE	W	L	SV	G	GS	IP	H	HR	BB/9	K/9	K	GB%	BABIP
2018	WSX	ROK	23	0	1	0	7	1	6^1	5	0	5.7	9.9	7	62.5%	.312
2019	KAN	LO-A	24	1	1	0	3	0	3	4	0	3.0	18.0	6	28.6%	.571
2019	BIR	AA	24	0	3	3	17	0	19^2	24	5	5.9	11.0	24	30.0%	.345
2020	CHW	MLB	25	0	1	0	8	0	7^1	11	4	3.7	13.5	11	39.1%	.368
2021 FS	CHW	MLB	26	2	2	0	57	0	50	44	7	4.7	10.2	56	39.3%	.291
2021 DC	CHW	MLB	26	1	1	0	31	0	16.7	15	2	4.7	10.2	19	39.3%	.291

Comparables: Joe Jiménez, Sam Tuivailala, Trevor Gott

    Four years after he was drafted—which is a little later than you envision for a decorated, first-round college closer—Burdi made his major league debut. Three years after his UCL put in for a sabbatical for recovery and self-discovery—which is longer than you envision for the grueling Tommy John surgery rehab, but not unprecedented—something resembling his old top shelf velocity returned, as he hit 99 mph frequently in major league games. And maybe it would be ideal for the White Sox pitching development if Burdi's return to top velocity and fluid delivery came purely through coaching and not Burdi saying he saw a video on Twitter and mimicked it. Even with all those qualifiers, Burdi made it back to the majors, he threw hard, he looked good, he flashed all three of his pitches and all was right in the world besides the fact that he got absolutely, relentlessly tattooed by major league hitting in his first turn.

YEAR	TEAM	LVL	AGE	WHIP	ERA	DRA-	WARP	MPH	FB%	WHF	CSP
2018	WSX	ROK	23	1.42	2.84						
2019	KAN	LO-A	24	1.67	9.00	58	0.1				
2019	BIR	AA	24	1.88	6.41	135	-0.5				
2020	CHW	MLB	25	1.91	11.05	89	0.1	99.1	50.0%	40.5%	
2021 FS	CHW	MLB	26	1.42	4.43	101	0.2	99.1	50.0%	40.5%	43.4%
2021 DC	CHW	MLB	26	1.42	4.43	101	0.1	99.1	50.0%	40.5%	43.4%

Zack Burdi, continued

Pitch Shape vs LHH

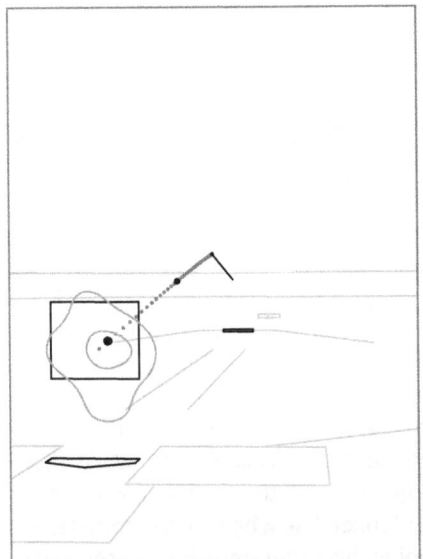

Pitch Shape vs RHH

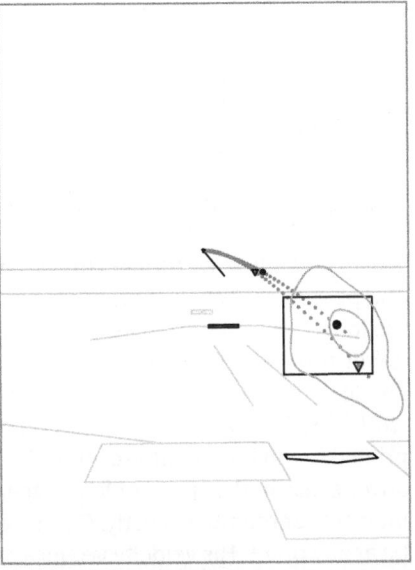

Type	Frequency	Velocity	H Movement	V Movement
● Fastball	50.0%	98 [117]	-10.1 [84]	-12.2 [108]
▲ Changeup	13.7%	91.3 [124]	-15.1 [82]	-23.7 [110]
▽ Slider	36.3%	88.5 [120]	2 [88]	-28 [117]

Chicago White Sox 2021

Dylan Cease   RHP
Born: 12/28/95   Age: 25   Bats: R   Throws: R
Height: 6'2"   Weight: 200   Origin: Round 6, 2014 Draft (#169 overall)

YEAR	TEAM	LVL	AGE	W	L	SV	G	GS	IP	H	HR	BB/9	K/9	K	GB%	BABIP
2018	WS	HI-A	22	9	2	0	13	13	71²	52	5	3.5	10.3	82	46.9%	.278
2018	BIR	AA	22	3	0	0	10	10	52¹	30	3	3.8	13.4	78	50.0%	.273
2019	CHA	AAA	23	5	2	0	15	15	68¹	75	4	4.2	9.5	72	53.1%	.372
2019	CHW	MLB	23	4	7	0	14	14	73	78	15	4.3	10.0	81	45.7%	.326
2020	CHW	MLB	24	5	4	0	12	12	58¹	50	12	5.2	6.8	44	39.8%	.239
2021 FS	CHW	MLB	25	9	9	0	26	26	150	138	22	5.0	8.9	147	42.9%	.285
2021 DC	CHW	MLB	25	7	7	0	24	24	123.7	114	18	5.0	8.9	122	42.9%	.285

Comparables: Reynaldo López, Mitch Keller, Tyler Mahle

The difference in attitudes toward major league-ready top pitching prospect and post-hype, below-average starting pitcher is stark, and yet Cease has made the journey in a mere 26 big league starts. Even finishing off an objectively poor debut season in 2019, he punctuated the year by overpowering a poor Tigers lineup, and looked dominant for stretches of spring training and summer workouts. So to alter the conception of his career from an immense talent primed for an imminent ascent took some doing, like issuing more walks than anyone else in the sport, or failing to record an out in the sixth inning in the month of September. Mostly, Cease never looked like who he was promised to be at any point. His velocity is overwhelming, his slider darts toward the earth like a meteor, but neither played like it against big league hitters, suggesting spin issues that need not just simple development to mature, but fundamental change.

YEAR	TEAM	LVL	AGE	WHIP	ERA	DRA-	WARP	MPH	FB%	WHF	CSP
2018	WS	HI-A	22	1.12	2.89	61	2.1				
2018	BIR	AA	22	0.99	1.72	58	1.6				
2019	CHA	AAA	23	1.57	4.48	92	1.5				
2019	CHW	MLB	23	1.55	5.79	108	0.4	98.2	51.5%	26.1%	
2020	CHW	MLB	24	1.44	4.01	157	-1.3	99.2	47.8%	25.3%	
2021 FS	CHW	MLB	25	1.47	4.70	105	1.1	98.7	49.5%	25.7%	42.2%
2021 DC	CHW	MLB	25	1.47	4.70	105	0.9	98.7	49.5%	25.7%	42.2%

Dylan Cease, *continued*

Pitch Shape vs LHH **Pitch Shape vs RHH**

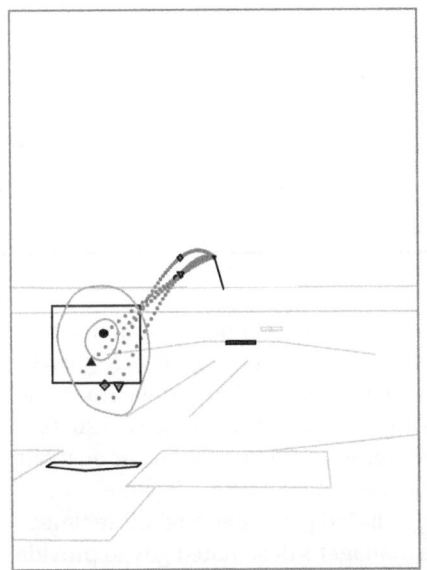 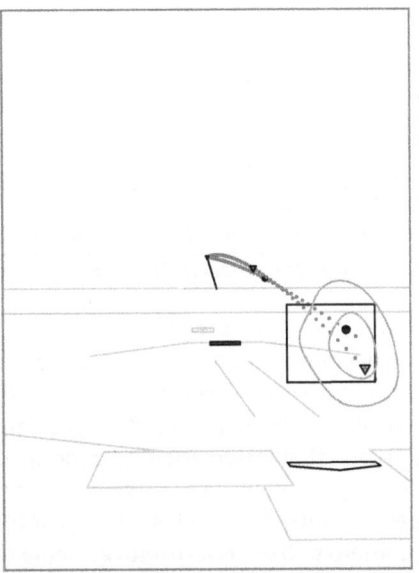

Type	Frequency	Velocity	H Movement	V Movement
● Fastball	47.7%	97.6 [116]	-3.8 [114]	-11.5 [110]
▲ Changeup	12.7%	83 [92]	-5.5 [133]	-22.3 [114]
▽ Slider	30.0%	85.2 [105]	6.3 [104]	-37.4 [89]
◇ Curveball	9.3%	79.1 [102]	6.7 [96]	-56.3 [82]

Jimmy Cordero   RHP
Born: 10/19/91   Age: 29   Bats: R   Throws: R
Height: 6'4"   Weight: 235   Origin: International Free Agent, 2012

YEAR	TEAM	LVL	AGE	W	L	SV	G	GS	IP	H	HR	BB/9	K/9	K	GB%	BABIP
2018	SYR	AAA	26	4	1	6	41	0	46	43	0	4.3	10.4	53	51.9%	.341
2018	WAS	MLB	26	1	2	0	22	0	19	23	2	5.7	5.7	12	57.4%	.318
2019	CHA	AAA	27	3	1	4	13	0	17^2	14	0	1.0	7.1	14	72.5%	.275
2019	FRE	AAA	27	0	1	3	12	0	15	17	3	5.4	10.2	17	53.3%	.333
2019	CHW	MLB	27	1	0	0	30	0	36	24	3	2.8	7.8	31	61.5%	.226
2019	TOR	MLB	27	0	1	0	1	0	1^1	2	1	0.0	0.0	0	40.0%	.250
2020	CHW	MLB	28	1	2	0	30	0	26^2	33	2	3.0	7.4	22	51.1%	.356
2021 FS	CHW	MLB	29	2	2	0	57	0	50	48	5	4.1	8.0	44	53.0%	.295
2021 DC	CHW	MLB	29	2	2	0	52	0	45	43	5	4.1	8.0	40	53.0%	.295

Comparables: Kevin McCarthy, Juan Minaya, Wander Suero

Once per year, a certain man is challenged to single-handedly demonstrate that if you throw an effective reliever over and over again, he gradually grows less effective. If we cheat and include the brief presence of the White Sox in the playoffs, Cordero managed to set a career-high with 32 appearances in 2020, in a season that lasted about two months. If that sounds like a lot on paper, it felt like he pitched in every single one. It's worth debating if a hot 30-game performance at the tail end of a year that included getting waived three times (Cordero's 2019), is as useful as being the manager's designated guy to provide increasingly mediocre innings when all other plans for the night have hit the rocks (his 2020). The latter endures the contempt of most onlookers in exchange for the appreciation of his most immediate supervisor. Then again, maybe he'll just stop getting cooked by left-handers if he figures out how to throw his changeup correctly again. Who can say?

YEAR	TEAM	LVL	AGE	WHIP	ERA	DRA-	WARP	MPH	FB%	WHF	CSP
2018	SYR	AAA	26	1.41	1.96	67	0.9				
2018	WAS	MLB	26	1.84	5.68	143	-0.3	100.2	61.7%	24.6%	
2019	CHA	AAA	27	0.91	0.51	44	0.7				
2019	FRE	AAA	27	1.73	6.00	87	0.3				
2019	CHW	MLB	27	0.97	2.75	71	0.7	99.8	68.6%	29.7%	
2019	TOR	MLB	27	1.50	6.75	127	0.0	98.1	53.3%	14.3%	
2020	CHW	MLB	28	1.57	6.08	94	0.3	98.6	68.9%	21.4%	
2021 FS	CHW	MLB	29	1.42	4.30	98	0.3	99.3	67.7%	25.0%	47.9%
2021 DC	CHW	MLB	29	1.42	4.30	98	0.3	99.3	67.7%	25.0%	47.9%

Jimmy Cordero, continued

Pitch Shape vs LHH

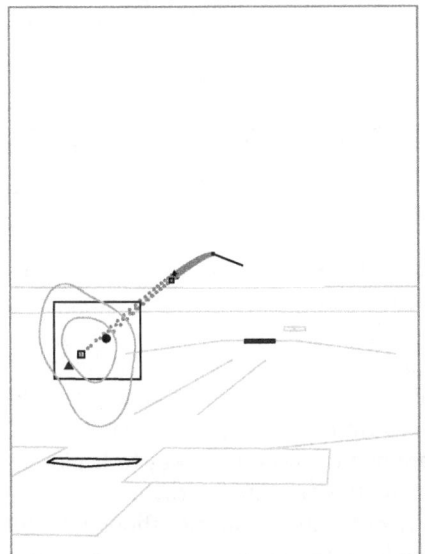

Pitch Shape vs RHH

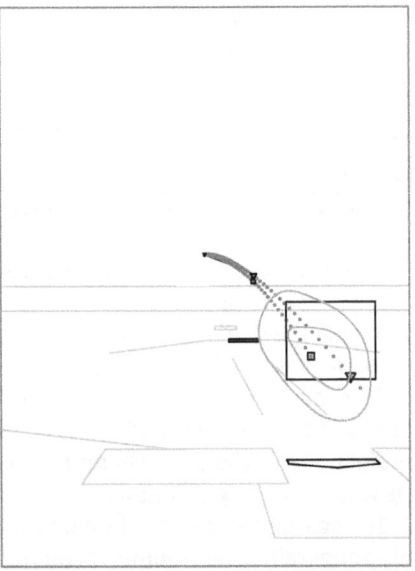

Type	Frequency	Velocity	H Movement	V Movement
● Fastball	9.6%	97.2 [115]	-4.3 [111]	-13.9 [104]
□ Sinker	58.5%	96.8 [122]	-12.9 [101]	-17 [111]
▲ Changeup	11.0%	88.7 [114]	-11.1 [103]	-24.4 [108]
▽ Slider	14.2%	88.4 [120]	1.3 [85]	-31.7 [106]
◇ Curveball	5.6%	84.2 [122]	2.7 [80]	-38.3 [122]

Matt Foster RHP

Born: 01/27/95   Age: 26   Bats: R   Throws: R
Height: 6'0"   Weight: 210   Origin: Round 20, 2016 Draft (#596 overall)

YEAR	TEAM	LVL	AGE	W	L	SV	G	GS	IP	H	HR	BB/9	K/9	K	GB%	BABIP
2018	WS	HI-A	23	2	1	7	21	0	28	25	1	2.2	12.9	40	42.9%	.400
2018	BIR	AA	23	0	4	1	24	0	32	33	3	3.7	8.4	30	42.1%	.326
2019	BIR	AA	24	0	0	1	6	0	9²	3	0	1.9	11.2	12	31.6%	.158
2019	CHA	AAA	24	4	1	4	37	0	55	46	9	3.1	10.1	62	35.9%	.280
2020	CHW	MLB	25	6	1	0	23	2	28²	16	2	2.8	9.7	31	34.8%	.212
2021 FS	CHW	MLB	26	2	2	0	57	0	50	43	8	3.4	10.0	55	36.6%	.279
2021 DC	CHW	MLB	26	2	2	0	52	0	56.3	48	9	3.4	10.0	62	36.6%	.279

Comparables: Trevor Kelley, Keith Butler, David Bednar

Foster is six feet tall, and no one would argue he's secretly six foot one, which is fairly short for a pitcher. He can rev it up to 94 mph out of the 'pen, which if watching the World Series is any indication, is hideously and embarrassingly slow. He was a 20th-round draft pick out of Alabama after two years in junior college, and in his single season at Tuscaloosa, he started zero games. He retired briefly at the start of the 2017 season, which would have been his first professional season, only to return and anonymously earn his way to Triple-A. He was a shocking addition to the White Sox 40-man roster in November of 2019, regarded as organizational filler by rival scouts and an afterthought for all of spring training and summer camp. Then he got called up and got people out, and kept doing it, unabated, all the way until the playoffs. He wiped out top-level hitters with a changeup he claims was taught to him full cloth by minor league pitching coach Matt Zaleski. Foster's story is one of incredible work ethic, perseverance, and Zaleski himself would point that his average velocity is countered by exceptional fastball carry, and that more raw ingredients of his changeup were present early in his career than he lets on. Still, many people are of the mind that plus relievers are indeed popping up out of literally nowhere, and Foster's emergence will only encourage them.

YEAR	TEAM	LVL	AGE	WHIP	ERA	DRA-	WARP	MPH	FB%	WHF	CSP
2018	WS	HI-A	23	1.14	2.57	66	0.6				
2018	BIR	AA	23	1.44	3.94	83	0.4				
2019	BIR	AA	24	0.52	0.00	46	0.3				
2019	CHA	AAA	24	1.18	3.76	60	1.8				
2020	CHW	MLB	25	0.87	2.20	90	0.4	95.2	57.2%	30.3%	
2021 FS	CHW	MLB	26	1.25	3.75	89	0.6	95.2	57.2%	30.3%	47.5%
2021 DC	CHW	MLB	26	1.25	3.75	89	0.7	95.2	57.2%	30.3%	47.5%

Matt Foster, continued

Pitch Shape vs LHH

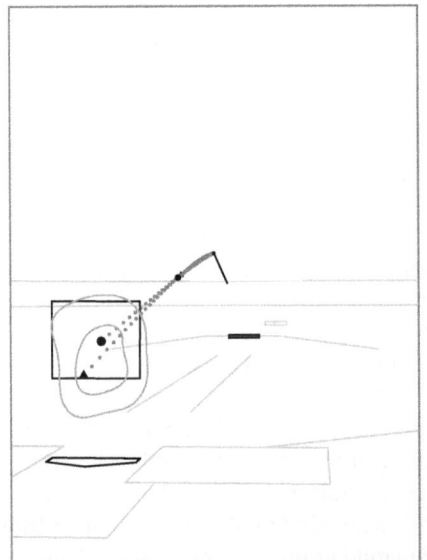

Pitch Shape vs RHH

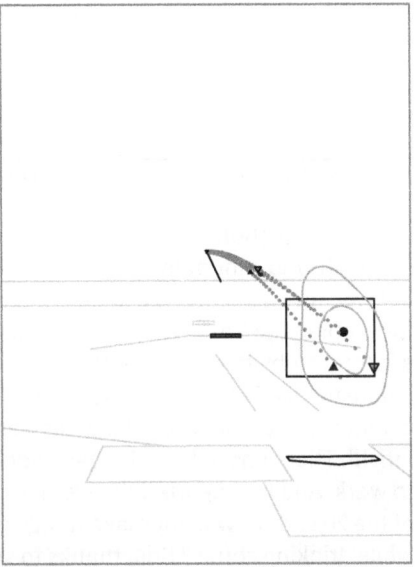

Type	Frequency	Velocity	H Movement	V Movement
● Fastball	57.1%	94 [104]	-6.9 [99]	-11.5 [110]
▲ Changeup	33.5%	83.9 [95]	-8.4 [118]	-22.8 [113]
▽ Slider	9.2%	85.5 [107]	2.8 [91]	-29.5 [112]

White Sox Player Analysis - 47

Jace Fry LHP

Born: 07/09/93   Age: 27   Bats: L   Throws: L
Height: 6'1"   Weight: 220   Origin: Round 3, 2014 Draft (#77 overall)

YEAR	TEAM	LVL	AGE	W	L	SV	G	GS	IP	H	HR	BB/9	K/9	K	GB%	BABIP
2018	CHA	AAA	24	0	0	0	5	0	6^2	3	1	0.0	14.8	11	53.8%	.167
2018	CHW	MLB	24	2	3	4	59	1	51^1	37	4	3.5	12.3	70	43.9%	.282
2019	CHW	MLB	25	3	4	0	68	0	55	44	7	7.0	11.1	68	56.9%	.289
2020	CHW	MLB	26	0	1	0	18	0	19^2	16	3	5.5	11.0	24	48.9%	.295
2021 FS	CHW	MLB	27	2	2	0	57	0	50	42	5	5.5	11.2	61	50.0%	.300
2021 DC	CHW	MLB	27	2	2	0	42	0	33.7	28	3	5.5	11.2	41	50.0%	.300

Comparables: Aaron Bummer, A.J. Minter, Anthony Banda

    In the collection of White Sox food last names, Fry is obviously primarily a side dish who cannot make the whole meal work on his own. Jake Burger being delayed for two seasons by Achilles tears and tendinitis is primarily responsible for keeping the Sox away from true transcendence on the diamond. It's certainly a factor in why the left-hander feels compelled to throw so many sliders. But a failure to take Seth Beer in the 2018 draft showed an inability or unwillingness to commit fully to the true ceiling of an entire brewpub menu in place on a single infield. There has to be full organizational commitment for something like this to work. And half-hearted efforts like selecting Adisyn Coffey in the third round of the 2020 draft will not make things right. What kind of life involves eating fries while drinking coffee? Still, thanks to some mild improvements in some truly awful 2019 control numbers, Fry will continue his wait in a major league bullpen, to be the finishing piece in a baseball-food last name pairing that will set Twitter ablaze for approximately 37 minutes during a single nationally televised White Sox game.

YEAR	TEAM	LVL	AGE	WHIP	ERA	DRA-	WARP	MPH	FB%	WHF	CSP
2018	CHA	AAA	24	0.45	1.35	36	0.3				
2018	CHW	MLB	24	1.11	4.38	66	1.2	95.2	34.3%	34.6%	
2019	CHW	MLB	25	1.58	4.75	83	0.8	94.4	25.1%	36.6%	
2020	CHW	MLB	26	1.42	3.66	88	0.3	92.0	38.9%	34.3%	
2021 FS	CHW	MLB	27	1.45	4.11	93	0.4	93.9	30.7%	35.6%	41.0%
2021 DC	CHW	MLB	27	1.45	4.11	93	0.3	93.9	30.7%	35.6%	41.0%

Jace Fry, continued

Pitch Shape vs LHH

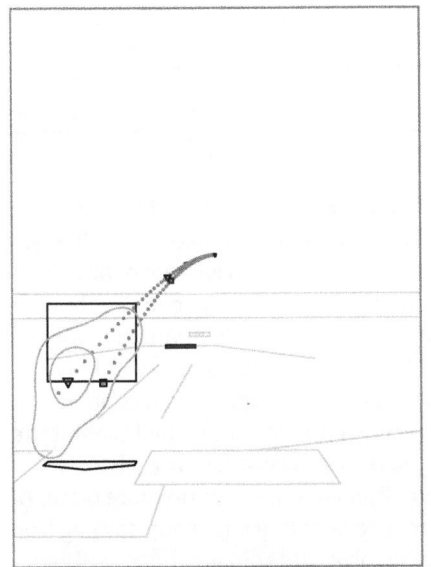

Pitch Shape vs RHH

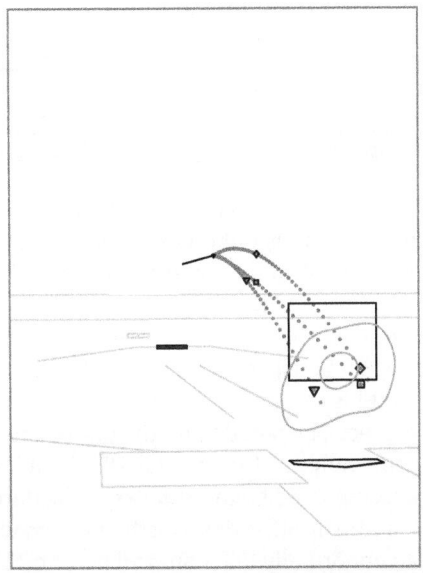

Type	Frequency	Velocity	H Movement	V Movement
● Fastball	9.5%	90.7 [94]	6.4 [101]	-16.4 [97]
□ Sinker	28.5%	89.7 [86]	10.8 [117]	-25.6 [84]
▲ Changeup	5.2%	85.7 [102]	11.3 [102]	-25.7 [105]
▽ Slider	37.5%	86.6 [112]	-0.7 [83]	-30.2 [110]
◇ Curveball	17.0%	76.6 [92]	-5.6 [92]	-52.6 [91]

Lucas Giolito   RHP

Born: 07/14/94   Age: 26   Bats: R   Throws: R
Height: 6'6"   Weight: 245   Origin: Round 1, 2012 Draft (#16 overall)

YEAR	TEAM	LVL	AGE	W	L	SV	G	GS	IP	H	HR	BB/9	K/9	K	GB%	BABIP
2018	CHW	MLB	23	10	13	0	32	32	173^1	166	27	4.7	6.5	125	44.4%	.269
2019	CHW	MLB	24	14	9	0	29	29	176^2	131	24	2.9	11.6	228	35.6%	.274
2020	CHW	MLB	25	4	3	0	12	12	72^1	47	8	3.5	12.1	97	43.5%	.255
2021 FS	CHW	MLB	26	10	7	0	26	26	150	122	21	3.8	11.2	186	41.0%	.285
2021 DC	CHW	MLB	26	11	8	0	29	29	174.7	142	25	3.8	11.2	217	41.0%	.285

Comparables: José Berríos, Tyler Mahle, Taijuan Walker

In 2019, Giolito completed one of the most stunning personal reinventions ever seen play out on the major league level. The way he remade his delivery, his arsenal, and his mental approach is a story to return to whenever anyone is weighing whether to give up on a talented, dedicated player, no matter how deep the struggles to get. The funny thing, though, is that lives aren't stories; at least not crisp, concise one with clear endings and morals. Giolito went home after his cathartic season and sought a way to follow it up. In most concrete respects, he failed to up the drama, producing a predictable sequel that hit the same notes as the original. His slight increase in strikeout rate was also accompanied by more walks, as he dared hitters to chase a little more often. At his core he still rides a fastball paired with a devastating changeup coming from an abnormally tall man, and his efforts to incorporate spin are mostly subplots. That he threw 2020's first no-hitter and took a perfect game into the seventh inning of his first playoff start doesn't mean a ton in terms of what kind of pitcher he is, but the highlights will get played over the credits of his still-incredible story.

YEAR	TEAM	LVL	AGE	WHIP	ERA	DRA-	WARP	MPH	FB%	WHF	CSP
2018	CHW	MLB	23	1.48	6.13	147	-2.5	94.8	59.5%	21.6%	
2019	CHW	MLB	24	1.06	3.41	57	5.7	96.4	55.0%	32.5%	
2020	CHW	MLB	25	1.04	3.48	76	1.6	96.1	50.6%	36.6%	
2021 FS	CHW	MLB	26	1.24	3.53	84	2.8	95.9	54.8%	31.1%	47.9%
2021 DC	CHW	MLB	26	1.24	3.53	84	3.3	95.9	54.8%	31.1%	47.9%

Lucas Giolito, continued

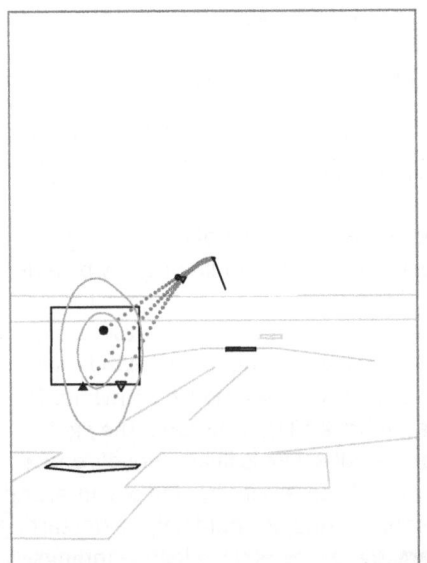
Pitch Shape vs LHH

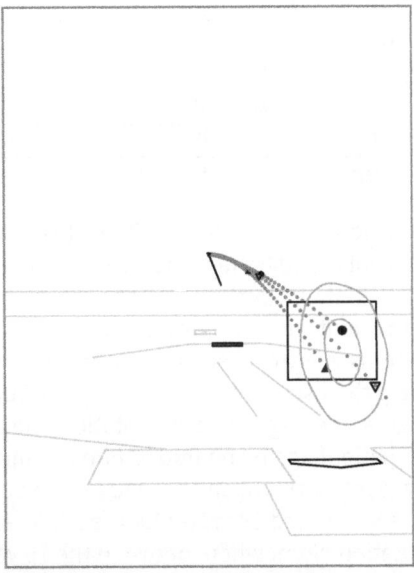
Pitch Shape vs RHH

Type	Frequency	Velocity	H Movement	V Movement
● Fastball	50.6%	94.2 [105]	-6.2 [102]	-11.1 [112]
▲ Changeup	33.6%	81 [84]	-7.7 [121]	-25.7 [105]
▽ Slider	14.8%	85.1 [105]	3.2 [92]	-30.4 [110]

Gio González LHP

Born: 09/19/85 Age: 35 Bats: R Throws: L
Height: 6'0" Weight: 205 Origin: Round 1, 2004 Draft (#38 overall)

YEAR	TEAM	LVL	AGE	W	L	SV	G	GS	IP	H	HR	BB/9	K/9	K	GB%	BABIP
2018	MIL	MLB	32	3	0	0	5	5	25^1	14	2	3.6	7.8	22	42.6%	.182
2018	WAS	MLB	32	7	11	0	27	27	145^2	153	15	4.3	7.8	126	45.5%	.321
2019	SWB	AAA	33	2	1	0	3	3	15	19	1	3.6	11.4	19	45.2%	.439
2019	MIL	MLB	33	3	2	0	19	17	87^1	76	9	3.8	8.0	78	44.6%	.282
2020	CHW	MLB	34	1	2	0	12	4	31^2	40	6	5.4	9.7	34	43.3%	.374
2021 FS	CHW	MLB	35	9	9	0	26	26	150	146	21	4.5	8.3	139	45.2%	.297

Comparables: Johnny Cueto, Clay Buchholz, Jordan Zimmermann

When the White Sox drafted a teenaged Gio González out of Hialeah High School in 2004, they did so with the expectation that he would one day be able to help their starting rotation. At the end of the 2005 season, they got a little impatient with waiting for him to be ready to do that and dealt him away. Jim Thome was involved. It made sense. A year later, while acquiring Gavin Floyd to help their starting rotation, they got González again. It seemed worthwhile. They figured he might help the rotation one day. A brisk 13 months later, they got impatient again and traded him in January of 2008. Life is fickle. Floyd's entire career has grown and eroded before our eyes, Thome is in the Hall of Fame, and the Sox added González for the 2020 season, figuring he could help their starting rotation. Somewhere between the 16 years, the over 1,900 big league innings, and the league shutting down for four months, the team underwent some reflection. González's shoulder aches frequently now, he cracks 90 mph infrequently, and his walk numbers resemble his prospect days in a bad way. Put on the spot, the Sox weren't convinced he could help their rotation, limiting him to a swingman role across 12 appearances.

YEAR	TEAM	LVL	AGE	WHIP	ERA	DRA-	WARP	MPH	FB%	WHF	CSP
2018	MIL	MLB	32	0.95	2.13	73	0.6	91.8	58.2%	29.1%	
2018	WAS	MLB	32	1.53	4.57	96	1.7	91.7	56.5%	23.1%	
2019	SWB	AAA	33	1.67	6.00	111	0.2				
2019	MIL	MLB	33	1.29	3.50	90	1.3	90.8	51.9%	26.0%	
2020	CHW	MLB	34	1.86	4.83	122	-0.1	91.6	47.0%	32.4%	
2021 FS	CHW	MLB	35	1.48	4.68	104	1.1	91.3	52.6%	26.8%	40.8%

Gio González, continued

Pitch Shape vs LHH

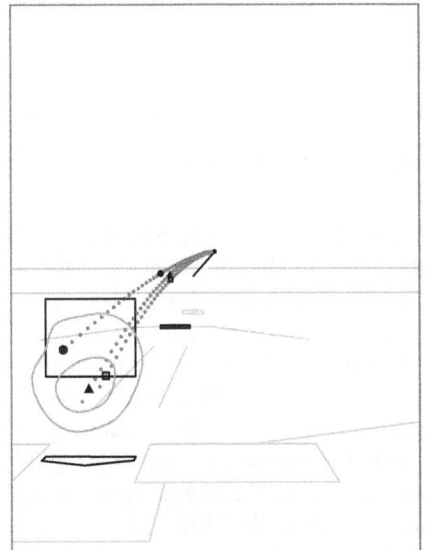

Pitch Shape vs RHH

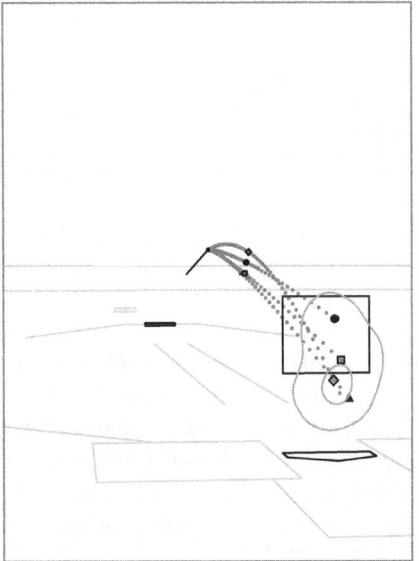

Type	Frequency	Velocity	H Movement	V Movement
● Fastball	33.3%	90.2 [92]	6.8 [99]	-16.1 [98]
□ Sinker	13.1%	89.4 [85]	12.9 [101]	-21.3 [98]
▲ Changeup	32.4%	83 [91]	11.7 [100]	-30.4 [92]
◇ Curveball	18.8%	76.8 [93]	-10.5 [112]	-54.8 [86]

Chicago White Sox 2021

Liam Hendriks   RHP

Born: 02/10/89   Age: 32   Bats: R   Throws: R
Height: 6'0"   Weight: 230   Origin: International Free Agent, 2007

YEAR	TEAM	LVL	AGE	W	L	SV	G	GS	IP	H	HR	BB/9	K/9	K	GB%	BABIP
2018	NAS	AAA	29	4	1	6	23	1	25¹	21	1	1.4	15.3	43	35.7%	.377
2018	OAK	MLB	29	0	1	0	25	8	24	25	3	3.8	8.2	22	39.4%	.324
2019	OAK	MLB	30	4	4	25	75	2	85	61	5	2.2	13.1	124	30.3%	.315
2020	OAK	MLB	31	3	1	14	24	0	25¹	14	1	1.1	13.1	37	28.8%	.260
2021 FS	CHW	MLB	32	3	2	32	57	0	50	39	7	2.2	12.0	66	35.1%	.287
2021 DC	CHW	MLB	32	3	2	32	65	0	56.3	44	8	2.2	12.0	75	35.1%	.287

Comparables: Tommy Hunter, Brett Cecil, Jeanmar Gómez

As fickle as relievers tend to be, Hendriks was eerily consistent between 2019 and 2020; his most notable change was dropping an already excellent WHIP by one-third, to an unfathomable 0.67. That and a 40-save pace earned Hendriks first-team All-MLB honors, a cool achievement even if it's not necessarily one a reader is likely to have heard of before this comment. Another sterling season also all-but ensured the pending free agent would be out of Oakland's price range, meaning you can make a little game out of the relievers surrounding Hendriks here: Who will be next season's out-of-nowhere relief ace on a highly affordable salary, whose simultaneous improvements in strikeout, walk, and hit rates confound hitters as much as evaluators? Wait for the buzzer to guess—*ding*

YEAR	TEAM	LVL	AGE	WHIP	ERA	DRA-	WARP	MPH	FB%	WHF	CSP
2018	NAS	AAA	29	0.99	2.84	48	0.8				
2018	OAK	MLB	29	1.46	4.12	104	0.1	97.2	70.1%	25.8%	
2019	OAK	MLB	30	0.96	1.80	56	2.4	98.6	70.6%	36.1%	
2020	OAK	MLB	31	0.67	1.78	66	0.7	97.8	70.5%	36.2%	
2021 FS	CHW	MLB	32	1.03	2.62	66	1.2	98.3	70.6%	35.0%	48.5%
2021 DC	CHW	MLB	32	1.03	2.62	66	1.4	98.3	70.6%	35.0%	48.5%

Liam Hendriks, continued

Pitch Shape vs LHH

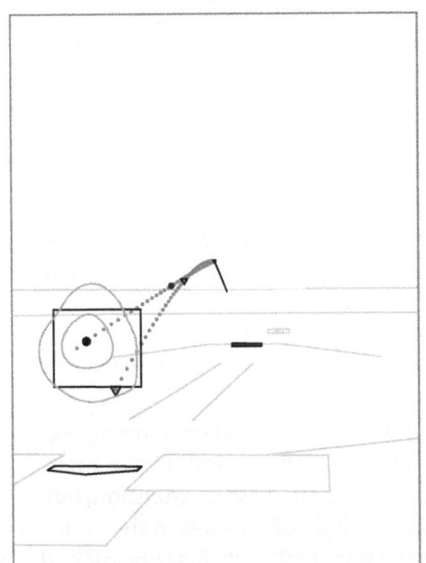

Pitch Shape vs RHH

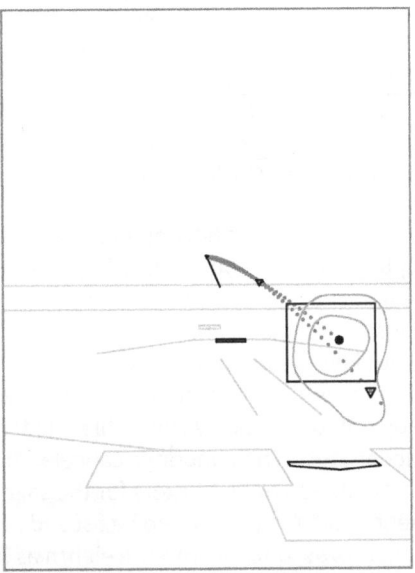

Type	Frequency	Velocity	H Movement	V Movement
● Fastball	69.5%	96.2 [111]	-7.1 [98]	-9.1 [117]
▽ Slider	21.9%	86.9 [113]	1.3 [85]	-30 [111]
◇ Curveball	7.0%	84.1 [121]	3.5 [83]	-45.8 [106]

Chicago White Sox 2021

Codi Heuer RHP
Born: 07/03/96 Age: 25 Bats: R Throws: R
Height: 6'5" Weight: 190 Origin: Round 6, 2018 Draft (#168 overall)

YEAR	TEAM	LVL	AGE	W	L	SV	G	GS	IP	H	HR	BB/9	K/9	K	GB%	BABIP
2018	GTF	ROK	21	0	1	0	14	14	38	49	4	3.3	8.3	35	56.3%	.369
2019	WS	HI-A	22	4	1	2	20	0	38^1	34	0	1.9	10.1	43	61.9%	.327
2019	BIR	AA	22	2	3	9	22	0	29^1	25	0	2.1	6.8	22	59.8%	.298
2020	CHW	MLB	23	3	0	1	21	0	23^2	12	1	3.4	9.5	25	50.0%	.193
2021 FS	CHW	MLB	24	2	2	0	57	0	50	45	6	4.1	8.3	46	51.2%	.282
2021 DC	CHW	MLB	24	2	2	0	52	0	56.3	51	7	4.1	8.3	52	51.2%	.282

Comparables: Alex Claudio, Michael Tonkin, Keynan Middleton

    There's a whole host of minor leaguers who were squeezed out of any real opportunity to demonstrate improvement in their craft enough to merit major league playing time in 2020. And then there was a host of guys who showed up for summer camp and, despite not having much experience, showed that it would be in everyone's best interest to just get the hell out of their way and let them play. Out of some broad coincidence, the latter group was largely populated by relievers who threw in the upper-90s with wild movement like Heuer touts. The pandemic canceled the 20 innings Heuer would have spent immolating Triple-A hitters for the sake of drawing his bosses' attention, but kept intact the part where he ascended up the chain of leverage in the White Sox relief corps, pitched into the eighth as his team locked up its first playoff berth in a dozen years, and factored heavily into their playoff series. In 2018, Heuer was a pretty bad starting pitcher in rookie ball. Some guys need years of minor league development, and some guys need a move to the 'pen, and a cut to the chase.

YEAR	TEAM	LVL	AGE	WHIP	ERA	DRA-	WARP	MPH	FB%	WHF	CSP
2018	GTF	ROK	21	1.66	4.74						
2019	WS	HI-A	22	1.10	2.82	73	0.5				
2019	BIR	AA	22	1.09	1.84	77	0.3				
2020	CHW	MLB	23	0.89	1.52	84	0.4	98.9	65.8%	33.9%	
2021 FS	CHW	MLB	24	1.37	4.02	94	0.4	98.9	65.8%	33.9%	45.6%
2021 DC	CHW	MLB	24	1.37	4.02	94	0.5	98.9	65.8%	33.9%	45.6%

Codi Heuer, continued

Pitch Shape vs LHH

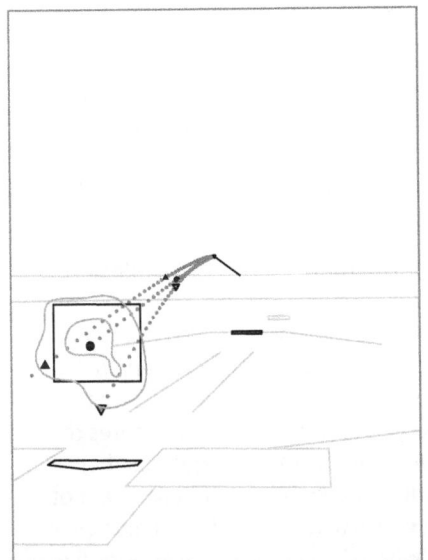

Pitch Shape vs RHH

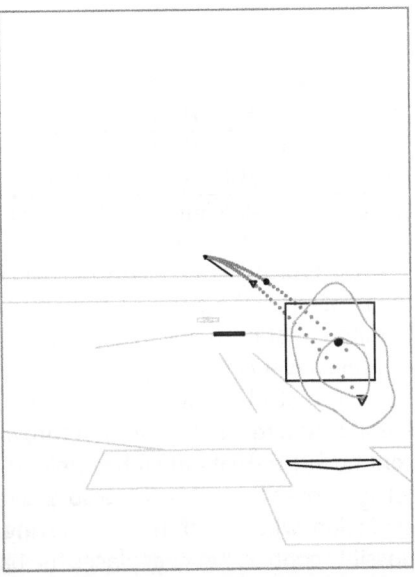

Type	Frequency	Velocity	H Movement	V Movement
● Fastball	65.6%	97.8 [117]	-13.3 [68]	-14.8 [101]
▲ Changeup	9.3%	89.3 [116]	-14.3 [87]	-24.6 [108]
▽ Slider	24.8%	88 [118]	3.3 [93]	-28.8 [114]

Dallas Keuchel LHP

Born: 01/01/88   Age: 33   Bats: L   Throws: L
Height: 6'2"   Weight: 220   Origin: Round 7, 2009 Draft (#221 overall)

YEAR	TEAM	LVL	AGE	W	L	SV	G	GS	IP	H	HR	BB/9	K/9	K	GB%	BABIP
2018	HOU	MLB	30	13	11	0	35	35	211^2	216	18	2.5	6.8	160	54.3%	.300
2019	ROM	LO-A	31	0	0	0	1	1	7	1	0	1.3	11.6	9	76.9%	.077
2019	MIS	AA	31	0	0	0	1	1	7	11	0	1.3	5.1	4	42.3%	.440
2019	ATL	MLB	31	8	8	0	19	19	112^2	115	16	3.1	7.3	91	58.3%	.303
2020	CHW	MLB	32	6	2	0	11	11	63^1	52	2	2.4	6.0	42	52.0%	.258
2021 FS	CHW	MLB	33	9	8	0	26	26	150	149	19	3.1	7.2	119	54.4%	.291
2021 DC	CHW	MLB	33	11	9	0	29	29	172	171	22	3.1	7.2	136	54.4%	.291

Comparables: Garrett Richards, Wade Miley, Homer Bailey

In the typical major league delivery of 2020, there's a point of explosion: a moment when the pitcher's body bursts forward through the path their front leg has already stalked out, and everything moves too fast to track in real time. Keuchel never gets blurry on the TV screen when he's pitching. Every inch of how far he strides toward home plate plays out smoothly visible in real time. Possibly as a result, he does not throw very hard and his velocity figures to continue its retreat until it has yielded every inch of major league-caliber territory over time. Possibly also as a result of never having that moment of explosion, where everything is moving too overwhelmingly fast in his delivery to possibly control, Keuchel places the ball where he wants. If that sounds like one notch above phrenology as analysis, it's this sort of belief in the ineffable that is required to see Keuchel's defiance of run estimators and the necessity of missing bats as something eternal and sustainable, rather than a brief marvel that should be celebrated for how long it has already managed to last.

YEAR	TEAM	LVL	AGE	WHIP	ERA	DRA-	WARP	MPH	FB%	WHF	CSP
2018	HOU	MLB	30	1.30	3.70	86	3.4	91.0	69.0%	19.8%	
2019	ROM	LO-A	31	0.29	0.00						
2019	MIS	AA	31	1.71	3.86	144	-0.2				
2019	ATL	MLB	31	1.37	3.75	87	1.9	89.9	74.0%	21.2%	
2020	CHW	MLB	32	1.09	1.99	99	0.6	88.9	65.5%	23.8%	
2021 FS	CHW	MLB	33	1.35	4.08	96	1.8	90.0	69.9%	21.5%	43.1%
2021 DC	CHW	MLB	33	1.35	4.08	96	2.1	90.0	69.9%	21.5%	43.1%

Dallas Keuchel, continued

Pitch Shape vs LHH
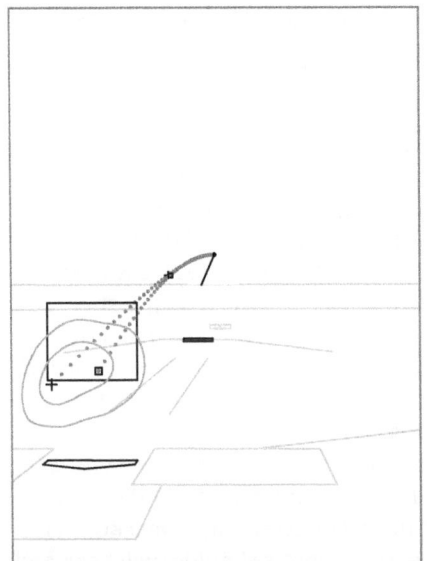

Pitch Shape vs RHH
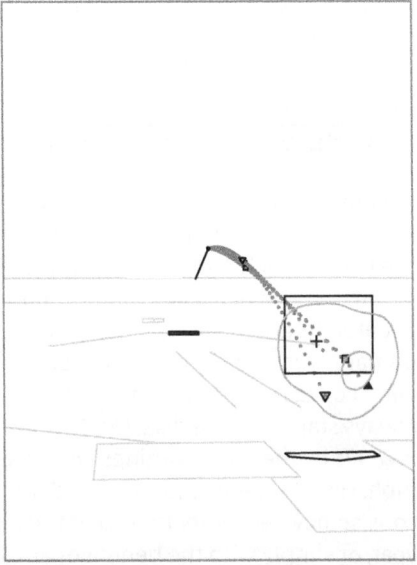

Type	Frequency	Velocity	H Movement	V Movement
☐ Sinker	32.5%	87.3 [74]	11.1 [114]	-25.8 [83]
+ Cutter	30.9%	84.9 [78]	-2.2 [102]	-26.6 [91]
▲ Changeup	27.9%	78.7 [75]	12.9 [94]	-33.6 [83]
▽ Slider	6.6%	76 [64]	-7 [106]	-43 [73]

Reynaldo López   RHP

Born: 01/04/94   Age: 27   Bats: R   Throws: R
Height: 6'1"   Weight: 220   Origin: International Free Agent, 2012

YEAR	TEAM	LVL	AGE	W	L	SV	G	GS	IP	H	HR	BB/9	K/9	K	GB%	BABIP
2018	CHW	MLB	24	7	10	0	32	32	188^2	165	25	3.6	7.2	151	33.0%	.260
2019	CHW	MLB	25	10	15	0	33	33	184	203	35	3.2	8.3	169	34.6%	.317
2020	CHW	MLB	26	1	3	0	8	8	26^1	28	9	5.1	8.2	24	33.3%	.268
2021 FS	CHW	MLB	27	9	9	0	26	26	150	143	27	3.9	8.5	142	34.9%	.282
2021 DC	CHW	MLB	27	6	4	0	48	6	71.7	68	13	3.9	8.5	68	34.9%	.282

Comparables: José Berríos, Zach Eflin, Daniel Mengden

From his first pitch of 2020, thrown in late July of this bizarre, accursed season, López never found the top-of-the-scale velocity that always served as the bedrock of his young career. He received a visit from the team's trainer before the end of his first inning, and soon after, an accompanying IL stint. Eventually, López would claim that the pain in his shoulder subsided, but the damage was done. What remained in its wake was an unflattering portrayal of what López has developed over the last few years alongside the velocity that always staved off the disaster. The mistakes he made while flagging into the low-90s by the end of outings were even more noticeable than they were at 96 mph. His changeup and slider had always had their moments, but the consistency necessary to pitch backward never surfaced. Maybe in a normal year, or simply with the benefit of an offseason, López's shoulder will heal, and the easy upper-90s will return. But even so, the same shortcomings will define his future.

YEAR	TEAM	LVL	AGE	WHIP	ERA	DRA-	WARP	MPH	FB%	WHF	CSP
2018	CHW	MLB	24	1.27	3.91	126	-0.7	98.0	60.9%	21.2%	
2019	CHW	MLB	25	1.46	5.38	144	-2.6	98.0	58.6%	24.7%	
2020	CHW	MLB	26	1.63	6.49	152	-0.5	96.0	51.4%	22.2%	
2021 FS	CHW	MLB	27	1.39	4.65	106	1.0	97.7	58.2%	23.4%	50.3%
2021 DC	CHW	MLB	27	1.39	4.65	106	0.4	97.7	58.2%	23.4%	50.3%

Reynaldo López, continued

Pitch Shape vs LHH

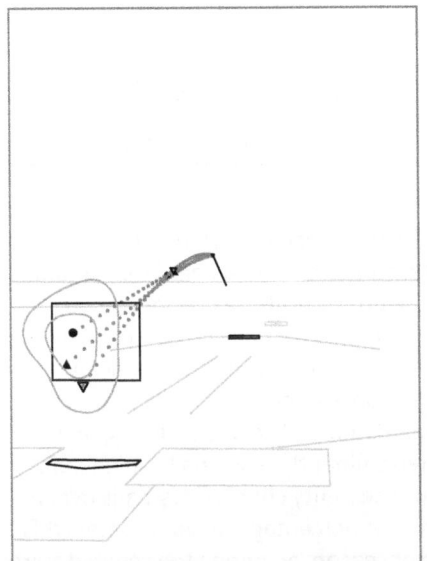

Pitch Shape vs RHH

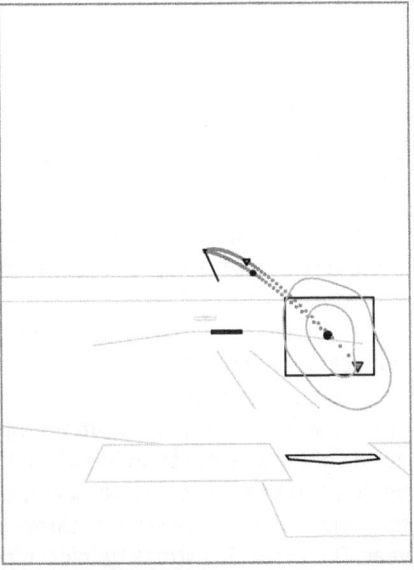

Type	Frequency	Velocity	H Movement	V Movement
● Fastball	51.4%	94.3 [105]	-6.3 [102]	-12.3 [108]
▲ Changeup	20.4%	83.7 [94]	-9.8 [110]	-24.1 [109]
▽ Slider	28.0%	82.1 [92]	4.1 [96]	-35.8 [94]

White Sox Player Analysis - 61

Lance Lynn RHP

Born: 05/12/87 Age: 34 Bats: S Throws: R
Height: 6'5" Weight: 250 Origin: Round 1, 2008 Draft (#39 overall)

YEAR	TEAM	LVL	AGE	W	L	SV	G	GS	IP	H	HR	BB/9	K/9	K	GB%	BABIP
2018	MIN	MLB	31	7	8	0	20	20	102[1]	105	12	5.5	8.8	100	51.2%	.322
2018	NYY	MLB	31	3	2	0	11	9	54[1]	58	2	2.3	10.1	61	47.4%	.364
2019	TEX	MLB	32	16	11	0	33	33	208[1]	195	21	2.5	10.6	246	39.9%	.322
2020	TEX	MLB	33	6	3	0	13	13	84	64	13	2.7	9.5	89	36.2%	.243
2021 FS	CHW	MLB	34	9	8	0	26	26	150	135	23	3.4	9.7	161	39.2%	.288
2021 DC	CHW	MLB	34	12	9	0	30	30	190.7	172	29	3.4	9.7	205	39.2%	.288

Comparables: Francisco Liriano, Jake Arrieta, Ian Kennedy

A couple notable things about Lynn's 2020 campaign: First, he threw a shutout with his razor, growing a majestic monstrosity of a beard that combined the woodsy-ness of Grizzly Adams with the unkempt-itude of Captain Lou Albano. It was truly a sight to behold. Second, and perhaps most importantly, Lynn cemented his status as one of the very best starters in the American League, giving up more than three runs just once in his first 12 starts, with an ERA a shade below 2.60, before the wheels completely came off in his final outing of the season. Lynn has always predominantly relied on his high-spin heater, and this season was no exception. The righty chucked fastballs over half the time, and only five starters threw a higher percentage of four seamers this year. The White Sox struck quickly in the offseason, acquiring the coveted starter to fortify their rotation for a potential playoff run.

YEAR	TEAM	LVL	AGE	WHIP	ERA	DRA	WARP	MPH	FB%	WHF	CSP
2018	MIN	MLB	31	1.63	5.10	123	-0.3	95.7	77.0%	23.7%	
2018	NYY	MLB	31	1.33	4.14	96	0.6	95.5	78.3%	23.5%	
2019	TEX	MLB	32	1.22	3.67	64	5.9	96.5	71.4%	28.6%	
2020	TEX	MLB	33	1.06	3.32	96	0.9	96.1	67.5%	25.4%	
2021 FS	CHW	MLB	34	1.28	3.95	92	2.1	96.2	71.5%	26.6%	48.2%
2021 DC	CHW	MLB	34	1.28	3.95	92	2.7	96.2	71.5%	26.6%	48.2%

Lance Lynn, continued

Pitch Shape vs LHH

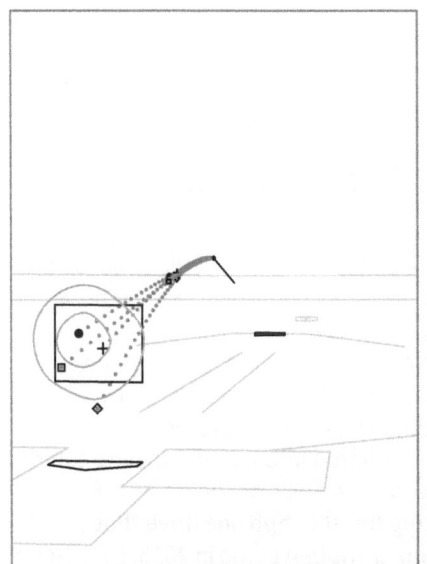

Pitch Shape vs RHH

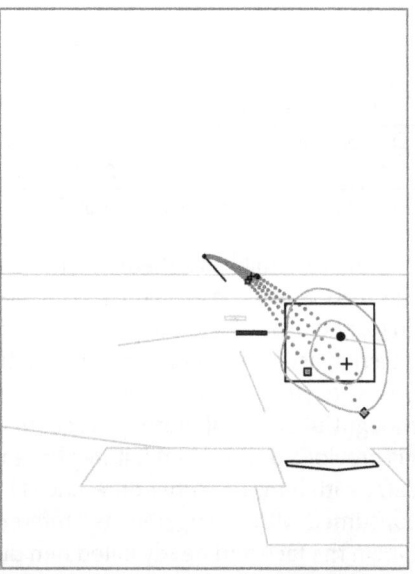

Type	Frequency	Velocity	H Movement	V Movement
● Fastball	49.0%	94.2 [105]	-5.9 [104]	-13.7 [104]
☐ Sinker	18.5%	92 [98]	-11.9 [109]	-22.5 [94]
+ Cutter	21.8%	89.7 [109]	1.6 [98]	-24 [101]
◇ Curveball	8.0%	83.5 [119]	4.2 [86]	-39.6 [120]

Evan Marshall RHP

Born: 04/18/90 Age: 31 Bats: R Throws: R
Height: 6'2" Weight: 235 Origin: Round 4, 2011 Draft (#124 overall)

YEAR	TEAM	LVL	AGE	W	L	SV	G	GS	IP	H	HR	BB/9	K/9	K	GB%	BABIP
2018	COL	AAA	28	1	1	4	20	0	24	18	1	1.1	7.9	21	66.2%	.258
2018	CLE	MLB	28	0	0	0	10	0	7	12	0	5.1	11.6	9	56.5%	.522
2019	CHA	AAA	29	3	0	2	9	0	10	8	0	0.9	11.7	13	43.5%	.364
2019	CHW	MLB	29	4	2	0	55	0	50^2	42	5	4.3	7.3	41	50.7%	.266
2020	CHW	MLB	30	2	1	0	23	0	22^2	17	1	2.8	11.9	30	53.6%	.291
2021 FS	CHW	MLB	31	2	2	1	57	0	50	44	5	3.7	9.6	53	50.8%	.292
2021 DC	CHW	MLB	31	2	2	1	52	0	50.7	44	5	3.7	9.6	53	50.8%	.292

Comparables: Javy Guerra, Ryan Webb, JC Ramírez

Evan Marshall has a theory he has shared a few times: He could always do this. He believes he always had the talent to be the shutdown reliever he was in 2020, and always had the physical ability. Despite velocity that he would describe as just fast enough to set up the rest of his arsenal, he could always post elite strikeout rates. The difference now is that he's smarter, more thoughtful and deliberate in his sequencing. The impacts and lessons of all of his previous outings and failures have materialized into a useful tool he could carry with him. The other difference Marshall cited was no longer being consumed with "flying objects," referencing the 105 mph line drive that struck him in the face and nearly killed him during a Triple-A game in 2015. He asserts that time has allowed him to pitch without being consumed by concern of a repeat. What a radical notion that our failures and traumas are not only recoverable, but just stepping stones on the path to our best selves. Only in baseball.

YEAR	TEAM	LVL	AGE	WHIP	ERA	DRA-	WARP	MPH	FB%	WHF	CSP
2018	COL	AAA	28	0.88	1.12	79	0.3				
2018	CLE	MLB	28	2.29	7.71	81	0.1	94.9	54.7%	33.8%	
2019	CHA	AAA	29	0.90	0.00	46	0.4				
2019	CHW	MLB	29	1.30	2.49	104	0.2	95.0	43.9%	24.6%	
2020	CHW	MLB	30	1.06	2.38	63	0.6	94.4	29.2%	34.7%	
2021 FS	CHW	MLB	31	1.30	3.65	87	0.6	94.7	38.8%	29.0%	41.4%
2021 DC	CHW	MLB	31	1.30	3.65	87	0.6	94.7	38.8%	29.0%	41.4%

Evan Marshall, continued

Pitch Shape vs LHH	Pitch Shape vs RHH
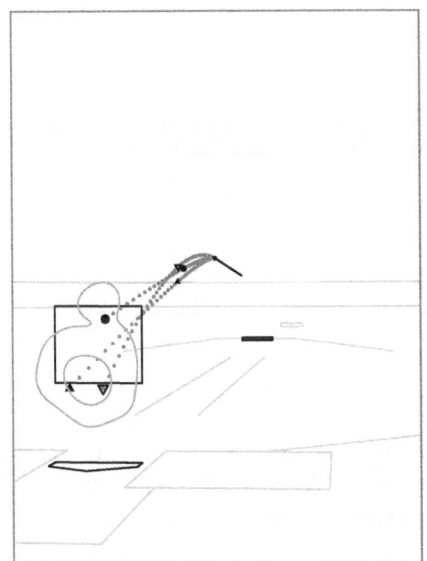	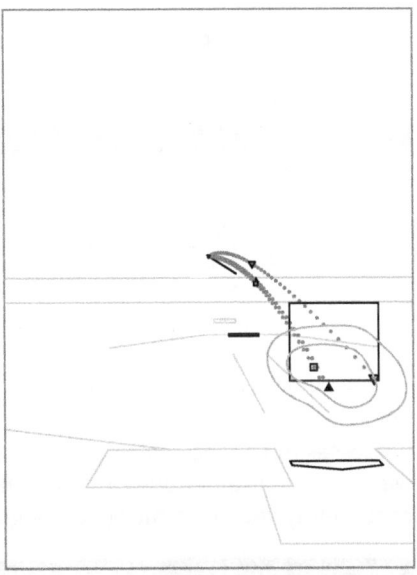

Type	Frequency	Velocity	H Movement	V Movement
● Fastball	17.1%	93.1 [102]	-9.1 [88]	-15.6 [99]
□ Sinker	11.9%	93.1 [103]	-14.3 [91]	-20.8 [99]
▲ Changeup	39.0%	87.9 [111]	-14.4 [86]	-28.1 [98]
▽ Slider	31.4%	82.3 [93]	7.4 [108]	-44.4 [69]

PLAYER COMMENTS WITHOUT GRAPHS

Micker Adolfo OF
Born: 09/11/96 Age: 24 Bats: R Throws: R
Height: 6'4" Weight: 240 Origin: International Free Agent, 2013

YEAR	TEAM	LVL	AGE	PA	R	2B	3B	HR	RBI	BB	K	SB	CS	AVG/OBP/SLG
2018	WS	HI-A	21	336	48	18	1	11	50	34	92	2	1	.282/.369/.464
2019	WSX	ROK	22	58	8	5	0	2	3	7	21	0	0	.260/.362/.480
2019	BIR	AA	22	95	5	7	0	0	9	14	36	0	3	.205/.337/.295
2021 FS	CHW	MLB	24	600	62	21	1	14	57	45	245	0	1	.187/.262/.314
2021 DC	CHW	MLB	24	67	7	2	0	1	6	5	27	0	0	.187/.262/.314

Comparables: Chris Parmelee, Alex Jackson, Scott Moore

The pandemic changed much about the fundamental nature of American life, but it left a writeup of Adolfo fundamentally unaltered. A big man who possesses top-of-the-scale raw power, he urgently needs a matured approach to wield it during games due to an unremarkable hit tool, and he cannot seem to consistently get into games to undergo that refinement.

YEAR	TEAM	LVL	AGE	PA	DRC+	BABIP	BRR	FRAA	WARP
2018	WS	HI-A	21	336	136	.372	-1.5		0.8
2019	WSX	ROK	22	58		.407			
2019	BIR	AA	22	95	95	.372	-0.3		0.3
2021 FS	CHW	MLB	24	600	57	.307	-0.8		-1.6
2021 DC	CHW	MLB	24	67	57	.307	-0.1	RF 0	-0.3

Zack Collins C
Born: 02/06/95 Age: 26 Bats: L Throws: R
Height: 6'3" Weight: 230 Origin: Round 1, 2016 Draft (#10 overall)

YEAR	TEAM	LVL	AGE	PA	R	2B	3B	HR	RBI	BB	K	SB	CS	AVG/OBP/SLG
2018	BIR	AA	23	531	58	24	1	15	68	101	158	5	0	.234/.382/.404
2019	CHA	AAA	24	367	56	19	1	19	74	62	98	0	0	.282/.403/.548
2019	CHW	MLB	24	102	10	3	1	3	12	14	39	0	0	.186/.307/.349
2020	CHW	MLB	25	18	1	1	0	0	2	5	0	0	0	.062/.167/.125
2021 FS	CHW	MLB	26	600	72	19	1	19	63	85	214	0	0	.194/.313/.356
2021 DC	CHW	MLB	26	126	15	3	0	4	13	17	44	0	0	.194/.313/.356

Comparables: Chris Carter, Dusty Ryan, Yasmani Grandal

The $3.4 million signing bonus that Collins received as the 10th-overall pick in 2016 probably keeps him from cracking any list of the top-10,000 people affected by the reduced major league season or the canceled minor league season. But save for 18 plate appearances and a three-pitch strikeout in the playoffs, one of the

YEAR	TEAM	P. COUNT	FRM RUNS	BLK RUNS	THRW RUNS	TOT RUNS
2018	BIR	10822	-12.2	-0.9	-0.7	-13.8
2019	CHW	1653	-1.8	-1.1	0.0	-2.9
2019	CHA	7026	-3.9	-0.1	-0.3	-4.3
2020	CHW	143	0.0	0.0		0.0
2021	CHW	6012	-5.0	-2.4	0.2	-7.2
2021	CHW	6012	-5.0	-3.2	0.2	-8.0

best catching situations in the league did not involve him, and he couldn't even crush Triple-A pitching again for old times' sake. No questions about his future were firmly answered in Schaumburg sim games, and all that the playoffs run provided were celebration videos that indicated his dancing is driven by makeup and want, rather than hip swivel.

YEAR	TEAM	LVL	AGE	PA	DRC+	BABIP	BRR	FRAA	WARP
2018	BIR	AA	23	531	124	.329	-3.2	C(74): -14.4	0.3
2019	CHA	AAA	24	367	133	.346	0.8	C(50): -4.6, 1B(20): -1.6	2.1
2019	CHW	MLB	24	102	78	.295	0.0	C(10): -3.0, 1B(1): -0.1	-0.3
2020	CHW	MLB	25	18	96	.091	0.2	C(2): -0.0, 1B(1): -0.0	0.0
2021 FS	CHW	MLB	26	600	87	.285	-0.7	C -26, 1B 0	-1.5
2021 DC	CHW	MLB	26	126	87	.285	-0.1	C -7	-0.6

Jarrod Dyson CF

Born: 08/15/84   Age: 36   Bats: L   Throws: R
Height: 5'9"   Weight: 165   Origin: Round 50, 2006 Draft (#1475 overall)

YEAR	TEAM	LVL	AGE	PA	R	2B	3B	HR	RBI	BB	K	SB	CS	AVG/OBP/SLG
2018	ARI	MLB	33	237	29	4	2	2	12	27	34	16	3	.189/.282/.257
2019	ARI	MLB	34	452	65	11	2	7	27	47	85	30	4	.230/.313/.320
2020	CHW	MLB	35	11	3	0	0	0	0	0	1	2	0	.300/.300/.300
2020	PIT	MLB	35	55	6	0	0	0	5	4	10	4	0	.157/.218/.157
2021 FS	CHW	MLB	36	600	53	19	2	9	52	51	114	42	10	.225/.301/.321

Comparables: Bill Bruton, Tom Goodwin, Cesar Geronimo

There is some element of Dyson's game that has steadily grown with his accumulation of knowledge. The sheer volume of pitcher deliveries he has watched, the catalogue of pick-off moves he has collected in his mind have built a compendium of information on how to run the bases that outpaces what his feet can deliver. His top speed at this point in life is slower than that of Eloy Jiménez, Nicky Delmonico, or simply the average major league player, and yet he's stolen 36 bases in 40 attempts over the last two seasons. At 36 years of age, he is physically slipping in a myriad of easily noticeable ways, and yet some part of him is rapidly getting better, almost keeping pace with the mounting limitations. It's a marvel worth celebrating, studying and commemorating. But since his bat is just fully cooked beyond belief as part of this, it's probably not worth rostering.

YEAR	TEAM	LVL	AGE	PA	DRC+	BABIP	BRR	FRAA	WARP
2018	ARI	MLB	33	237	70	.216	2.6	CF(41): 3.3, RF(18): 0.0, LF(6): 1.1	0.6
2019	ARI	MLB	34	452	77	.274	6.3	CF(103): -3.7, RF(21): 4.0, LF(16): 0.0	0.8
2020	CHW	MLB	35	11	75	.333	0.1	LF(6): -0.1, CF(2): -0.2, RF(1): 0.1	-0.1
2020	PIT	MLB	35	55	79	.195	0.4	CF(21): 0.0	0.1
2021 FS	CHW	MLB	36	600	74	.269	3.5	CF 3, RF 1	0.5

Luis González CF

Born: 09/10/95 Age: 25 Bats: L Throws: L
Height: 6'1" Weight: 180 Origin: Round 3, 2017 Draft (#87 overall)

YEAR	TEAM	LVL	AGE	PA	R	2B	3B	HR	RBI	BB	K	SB	CS	AVG/OBP/SLG
2018	KAN	LO-A	22	255	35	16	2	8	26	21	57	7	2	.300/.358/.491
2018	WS	HI-A	22	288	50	24	3	6	45	27	46	3	5	.313/.376/.504
2019	BIR	AA	23	535	63	18	4	9	59	47	89	17	9	.247/.316/.359
2020	CHW	MLB	24	2	1	0	0	0	0	0	1	0	0	.000/.500/.000
2021 FS	CHW	MLB	25	600	58	23	3	16	64	46	154	4	3	.226/.290/.370

Comparables: Braxton Lee, Roger Bernadina, Rey Fuentes

The first ball hit to González in the outfield as a major leaguer struck the heel of his glove and dropped to the grass. His only time on base on record came on a hit by pitch. But even working his way up to emergency reserve represents an upgrade over the way González's 2019 ended in Double-A Birmingham.

YEAR	TEAM	LVL	AGE	PA	DRC+	BABIP	BRR	FRAA	WARP
2018	KAN	LO-A	22	255	144	.365	-0.6	CF(39): -1.0, RF(13): -1.9	1.1
2018	WS	HI-A	22	288	145	.354	5.8	CF(31): 3.9, LF(14): 0.2, RF(12): -0.6	2.5
2019	BIR	AA	23	535	103	.281	1.0	CF(60): 0.7, RF(29): 1.1, LF(20): 2.0	2.1
2020	CHW	MLB	24	2	81		0.1	LF(1): -0.0, CF(1): -0.0	0.0
2021 FS	CHW	MLB	25	600	82	.283	0.0	CF 4, RF 2	1.1

Chicago White Sox 2021

Yermín Mercedes C
Born: 02/14/93   Age: 28   Bats: R   Throws: R
Height: 5'11"   Weight: 235   Origin: International Free Agent, 2011

YEAR	TEAM	LVL	AGE	PA	R	2B	3B	HR	RBI	BB	K	SB	CS	AVG/OBP/SLG
2018	WS	HI-A	25	410	58	24	1	14	64	40	67	4	0	.289/.362/.478
2019	BIR	AA	26	167	19	7	0	6	18	17	25	2	0	.327/.389/.497
2019	CHA	AAA	26	220	35	12	0	17	62	24	42	0	0	.310/.386/.647
2020	CHW	MLB	27	1	0	0	0	0	0	0	0	0	0	.000/.000/.000
2021 FS	CHW	MLB	28	600	81	25	1	28	85	47	144	0	0	.260/.324/.471
2021 DC	CHW	MLB	28	33	4	1	0	1	4	2	7	0	0	.260/.324/.471

Comparables: Ryan Doumit, Travis d'Arnaud, Tim Federowicz

As a power-hitting, big leg-kicking, rollie pollie of a baseball player, Mercedes has always come across as better suited to legend than a projectable member of a major league roster. Apparently the White Sox agreed, marooning Mercedes to either the alternate site in Schaumburg, or as a particularly ebullient member of the traveling taxi squad. As such, Mercedes lives on in memory as the guy who hit the crap out of everything during intrasquad games and sputtered around the bases joyfully. Never was he submitted to questions like "Oh boy, we're not really sure if this guy can catch, are we?" or "He really not very fast, is he?" or "Jeez, why did he do that?" and everyone is the better for it. Well, except for Mercedes, perhaps, who likely can hit at a major league proficiency and, at 28 years of age, would like to get paid for it at some point. To that end, well, who knows? Being interesting and cool does not always equate to a team allotting hundreds of plate appearances to a catcher/DH/first base/third base/left field hybrid, and even all the Willians Astudillo hype never materialized into steady work. Legends live forever, though.

YEAR	TEAM	LVL	AGE	PA	DRC+	BABIP	BRR	FRAA	WARP
2018	WS	HI-A	25	410	146	.317	0.1	C(78): 1.4, 1B(14): -0.6	2.9
2019	BIR	AA	26	167	166	.353	-0.8	C(34): 6.7	2.5
2019	CHA	AAA	26	220	142	.306	-2.4	C(24): 3.2, 1B(4): -0.6, 3B(2): -0.3	1.6
2020	CHW	MLB	27	1	82	.000			0.0
2021 FS	CHW	MLB	28	600	115	.305	-0.9	C 8, 1B 0	4.2
2021 DC	CHW	MLB	28	33	115	.305	-0.1	C 1	0.3

Blake Rutherford RF

Born: 05/02/97 Age: 24 Bats: L Throws: R
Height: 6'3" Weight: 210 Origin: Round 1, 2016 Draft (#18 overall)

YEAR	TEAM	LVL	AGE	PA	R	2B	3B	HR	RBI	BB	K	SB	CS	AVG/OBP/SLG
2018	WS	HI-A	21	487	67	25	9	7	78	34	90	15	8	.293/.345/.436
2019	BIR	AA	22	480	50	17	3	7	49	37	117	9	2	.265/.319/.365
2021 FS	CHW	MLB	24	600	62	21	4	11	60	41	172	4	2	.223/.279/.339
2021 DC	CHW	MLB	24	33	3	1	0	0	3	2	9	0	0	.223/.279/.339

Comparables: Jorge Bonifacio, Daniel Johnson, Bronson Sardinha

People in the White Sox organization say Rutherford tapped into his power at long last during his unrecorded, unbroadcasted alternate site simulated games. It seems convenient that the fundamental question hanging over Rutherford's increasingly platoon-corner-outfield profile was answered by a method that no one could independently verify, but from the perspective of assessing his trade value or immediate major-league viability, it's not very convenient at all.

YEAR	TEAM	LVL	AGE	PA	DRC+	BABIP	BRR	FRAA	WARP
2018	WS	HI-A	21	487	120	.351	1.1	RF(73): -2.5, LF(15): -2.7, CF(13): -1.4	0.4
2019	BIR	AA	22	480	95	.342	2.4	RF(68): 1.7, LF(29): -1.7, CF(1): -0.1	1.0
2021 FS	CHW	MLB	24	600	70	.302	0.1	LF -9, CF 0	-1.9
2021 DC	CHW	MLB	24	33	70	.302	0.0	LF 0	-0.1

Gavin Sheets 1B

Born: 04/23/96 Age: 25 Bats: L Throws: L
Height: 6'5" Weight: 245 Origin: Round 2, 2017 Draft (#49 overall)

YEAR	TEAM	LVL	AGE	PA	R	2B	3B	HR	RBI	BB	K	SB	CS	AVG/OBP/SLG
2018	WS	HI-A	22	497	58	28	2	6	61	52	81	1	0	.293/.368/.407
2019	BIR	AA	23	527	56	18	1	16	83	54	99	3	1	.267/.345/.414
2021 FS	CHW	MLB	25	600	68	23	1	16	67	49	143	0	0	.241/.309/.380
2021 DC	CHW	MLB	25	33	3	1	0	0	3	2	7	0	0	.241/.309/.380

Comparables: Andy Wilkins, Chris Parmelee, Will Craig

If one look at Sheets' hulking, muscled frame doesn't give away what role he is seeking to fill at the major league level, a five-minute look at his best left-handed power strokes in a batting practice session should settle the matter. But at this point, the professional resumé consists of a few months at Double-A Birmingham in 2019 where he looked the part, buried amid power outages and an Arizona Fall League showing that nibble away at the viability of such a bat-first profile.

Chicago White Sox 2021

YEAR	TEAM	LVL	AGE	PA	DRC+	BABIP	BRR	FRAA	WARP
2018	WS	HI-A	22	497	131	.344	-3.9	1B(107): -4.3	0.3
2019	BIR	AA	23	527	128	.305	-6.3	1B(110): 3.8	1.9
2021 FS	*CHW*	*MLB*	*25*	*600*	*90*	*.298*	*-0.8*	*1B 1*	*0.1*
2021 DC	*CHW*	*MLB*	*25*	*33*	*90*	*.298*	*0.0*	*1B 0*	*0.0*

Preston Tucker LF
Born: 07/06/90 Age: 31 Bats: L Throws: L
Height: 6'0" Weight: 210 Origin: Round 7, 2012 Draft (#219 overall)

YEAR	TEAM	LVL	AGE	PA	R	2B	3B	HR	RBI	BB	K	SB	CS	AVG/OBP/SLG
2018	GWN	AAA	27	62	7	4	1	0	6	2	5	0	0	.250/.274/.350
2018	ATL	MLB	27	142	15	10	0	4	22	9	34	0	0	.240/.303/.411
2018	CIN	MLB	27	42	4	1	0	2	5	4	9	0	0	.189/.286/.378
2019	CHA	AAA	28	93	14	8	0	1	10	9	7	0	1	.277/.344/.410
2019	KIA	KBO	28	399	50	33	0	9	50	38	44	0	0	.311/.381/.479
2020	KIA	KBO	29	631	100	40	0	32	113	76	67	0	2	.306/.398/.557
2021 FS	*CHW*	*MLB*	*30*	*600*	*61*	*26*	*2*	*19*	*68*	*49*	*155*	*0*	*1*	*.217/.289/.383*

Comparables: Mike Colangelo, Ryan Rua, Jon Knott

"Hit a car, win the car" is the rule of the game at Gwangju Kia Champions Field, and Tucker earned a bit of notoriety by denting the Kia Sorrento perched atop the right field pavilion last May. In his first full season in Tigers colors, Tucker and his amusingly tiny batting helmet torched the league. His OPS was good for fifth in the league, all the more impressive considering his cavernous home park. The 30-year-old has all of the physical skills you normally find in a big-league regular; his one fatal flaw is that he can't *not* swing at the high cheese. Major-league pitchers figured this out quickly enough, and ate him alive with heaters up, well out of the zone. But while he swung and missed at that pitch in the states, KBO pitchers don't throw quite so hard, and all of those empty hacks turned into foul balls over in Korea. Eventually they threw something else, often to their detriment. If he can keep from scratching the big-league itch, he'll rake in Asia for as long as he wants.

YEAR	TEAM	LVL	AGE	PA	DRC+	BABIP	BRR	FRAA	WARP
2018	GWN	AAA	27	62	72	.273	0.4	LF(14): 0.1	-0.1
2018	ATL	MLB	27	142	85	.293	0.4	LF(27): 1.2, RF(4): -0.2	0.3
2018	CIN	MLB	27	42	90	.192	-0.2	LF(10): -2.6	-0.2
2019	CHA	AAA	28	93	98	.289	-0.6	LF(14): -0.4, RF(3): 0.0	0.1
2019	KIA	KBO	28	399					
2020	KIA	KBO	29	631					
2021 FS	*CHW*	*MLB*	*30*	*600*	*82*	*.266*	*-0.7*	*LF 2, RF 0*	*0.3*

Andrew Vaughn 1B

Born: 04/03/98   Age: 23   Bats: R   Throws: R
Height: 6'0"   Weight: 215   Origin: Round 1, 2019 Draft (#3 overall)

YEAR	TEAM	LVL	AGE	PA	R	2B	3B	HR	RBI	BB	K	SB	CS	AVG/OBP/SLG
2019	WSX	ROK	21	16	3	2	0	1	4	0	3	0	0	.600/.625/.933
2019	KAN	LO-A	21	103	14	7	0	2	11	14	18	0	0	.253/.388/.410
2019	WS	HI-A	21	126	16	8	0	3	21	16	17	0	1	.252/.349/.411
2021 FS	CHW	MLB	23	600	63	24	1	11	59	44	149	0	1	.220/.289/.335
2021 DC	CHW	MLB	23	398	42	16	1	7	39	29	98	0	0	.220/.289/.335

Comparables: Nick Evans, Max Muncy, Daniel Vogelbach

The baseball viewing public's interest in Vaughn, an ivory-colored bowling ball of a man, fails to stretch far beyond his predilection for studiously drilling fastballs to right field and dragging his barrel to flick off speed to left field, all with the requisite strength of a highly sentient bowling ball. From anecdotal observations of a summer of simulated games and multiple stretches in big league training camp, Vaughn continued to play his part with the consistency of a bowling ball rolling down a smoothened ramp. To spice things up, the White Sox had Vaughn get some work at third base and right field, which do not seem like ideal roles for a bowling ball. But a bowling ball with an expanded skill set seems fascinating.

YEAR	TEAM	LVL	AGE	PA	DRC+	BABIP	BRR	FRAA	WARP
2019	WSX	ROK	21	16		.727			
2019	KAN	LO-A	21	103	137	.297	1.2	1B(19): -0.5	0.6
2019	WS	HI-A	21	126	139	.270	-0.3	1B(16): -0.3	0.5
2021 FS	CHW	MLB	23	600	73	.283	-0.8	1B -1	-1.4
2021 DC	CHW	MLB	23	398	73	.283	-0.6	1B -1	-0.9

Nick Williams LF

Born: 09/08/93   Age: 27   Bats: L   Throws: L
Height: 6'3"   Weight: 208   Origin: Round 2, 2012 Draft (#93 overall)

YEAR	TEAM	LVL	AGE	PA	R	2B	3B	HR	RBI	BB	K	SB	CS	AVG/OBP/SLG
2018	PHI	MLB	24	448	53	12	3	17	50	32	111	3	2	.256/.324/.425
2019	LHV	AAA	25	210	33	15	2	10	25	14	52	1	0	.316/.381/.574
2019	PHI	MLB	25	112	9	4	0	2	5	4	43	0	0	.151/.196/.245
2021 FS	CHW	MLB	27	600	64	26	3	21	74	36	180	1	2	.241/.300/.421

Comparables: Doug Frobel, Jayson Werth, Byron Browne

Williams is a poor corner outfielder who strikes out a ton, but he's only 27, has some skill with the bat, was once a top prospect and has put up perfectly acceptable numbers whenever he's received consistent playing time; there might still be something here.

Chicago White Sox 2021

YEAR	TEAM	LVL	AGE	PA	DRC+	BABIP	BRR	FRAA	WARP
2018	PHI	MLB	24	448	98	.312	-1.4	RF(95): -9.8, LF(19): -1.5	-0.4
2019	LHV	AAA	25	210	130	.391	1.4	LF(20): 1.2, CF(16): 1.0, RF(11): 1.8	1.7
2019	PHI	MLB	25	112	45	.230	0.4	LF(23): 0.0, RF(5): -0.3	-0.4
2021 FS	CHW	MLB	27	600	93	.318	-0.4	RF -2, LF 0	0.6

Seby Zavala   C
Born: 08/28/93   Age: 27   Bats: R   Throws: R
Height: 5'11"   Weight: 210   Origin: Round 12, 2015 Draft (#352 overall)

YEAR	TEAM	LVL	AGE	PA	R	2B	3B	HR	RBI	BB	K	SB	CS	AVG/OBP/SLG
2018	BIR	AA	24	232	32	7	0	11	31	27	65	0	0	.271/.358/.472
2018	CHA	AAA	24	191	18	15	0	2	20	6	44	0	2	.243/.267/.359
2019	CHA	AAA	25	331	49	14	0	20	45	26	116	1	1	.222/.296/.471
2019	CHW	MLB	25	12	1	0	0	0	0	0	9	0	0	.083/.083/.083
2021 FS	CHW	MLB	27	600	62	18	1	16	59	42	219	0	0	.191/.258/.320
2021 DC	CHW	MLB	27	31	3	0	0	0	3	2	11	0	0	.191/.258/.320

Comparables: Cameron Rupp, Kyle Skipworth, Chad Santos

Optimism that Zavala's raw pop would wriggle its way into big league games has been in short supply since he hit Triple-A. But a team that had two All-Stars, a former 10th-overall pick, and a guy who posted 1.047 OPS in their catching depth still insisted on carrying Zavala as the *fifth* catcher on their 40-man roster for an entire calendar year, so perhaps the savvy game-caller has qualities that can't be easily appreciated from the outside.

YEAR	TEAM	P. COUNT	FRM RUNS	BLK RUNS	THRW RUNS	TOT RUNS
2018	CHA	4736	-2.6	0.0	-0.1	-2.8
2018	BIR	4315	3.3	0.1	0.4	3.8
2019	CHW	345	0.1	0.1	0.0	0.2
2019	CHA	7394	5.4	-0.1	0.4	5.8
2021	CHW	2405	0.9	0.8	-0.2	1.5
2021	CHW	2405	0.9	-4.1	-0.2	-3.4

YEAR	TEAM	LVL	AGE	PA	DRC+	BABIP	BRR	FRAA	WARP
2018	BIR	AA	24	232	132	.339	0.0	C(31): 4.0	1.5
2018	CHA	AAA	24	191	81	.304	-1.2	C(35): -3.0	-0.4
2019	CHA	AAA	25	331	77	.282	-1.7	C(52): 6.8, 1B(18): -0.3	0.7
2019	CHW	MLB	25	12	51	.333	0.0	C(3): 0.2	0.0
2021 FS	CHW	MLB	27	600	56	.282	-0.9	C 22, 1B 0	1.1
2021 DC	CHW	MLB	27	31	56	.282	0.0	C 1	0.1

Garrett Crochet LHP

Born: 06/21/99   Age: 22   Bats: L   Throws: L
Height: 6'6"   Weight: 218   Origin: Round 1, 2020 Draft (#11 overall)

YEAR	TEAM	LVL	AGE	W	L	SV	G	GS	IP	H	HR	BB/9	K/9	K	GB%	BABIP
2020	CHW	MLB	21	0	0	0	5	0	6	3	0	0.0	12.0	8	61.5%	.231
2021 FS	CHW	MLB	22	9	8	0	26	26	150	145	22	3.6	8.2	137	44.9%	.290
2021 DC	CHW	MLB	22	0	0	0	9	0	45	43	6	3.6	8.2	41	44.9%	.290

Comparables: Jesús Luzardo, Caleb Ferguson, Luiz Gohara

For someone who threw 10 innings on record in between two separate injuries, Crochet had a rollicking good time of a season. He got drafted 11th overall in June, he got millions of dollars, he got called up to the majors in September, he got to 100 mph with the fastball regularly, and got to taste postseason baseball. That triple-digit heater with ride hisses like a menacing snake. It's impressive, even jarring on sight. And as a result, so is Crochet. He coils his left forearm close to his shoulder, unfurls and hisses, and it's stunning to imagine what he could be. It's also just a flash, since between his shoulder aching and COVID-19 he had one outing for his junior season at Tennessee and left Game 3 of the Wild Card Series with a forearm strain. At a certain point, injuries become part of the story, not just what keeps it shrouded in mystery. Crochet has shown that in equal portion with his pyrotechnics, but the hissing lingers longer in memory.

YEAR	TEAM	LVL	AGE	WHIP	ERA	DRA-	WARP	MPH	FB%	WHF	CSP
2020	CHW	MLB	21	0.50	0.00	81	0.1	101.6	84.7%	40.5%	
2021 FS	CHW	MLB	22	1.37	4.46	103	1.2	101.6	84.7%	40.5%	48.9%
2021 DC	CHW	MLB	22	1.37	4.46	103	0.1	101.6	84.7%	40.5%	48.9%

Andrew Dalquist RHP

Born: 11/13/00   Age: 20   Bats: R   Throws: R
Height: 6'1"   Weight: 175   Origin: Round 3, 2019 Draft (#81 overall)

YEAR	TEAM	LVL	AGE	W	L	SV	G	GS	IP	H	HR	BB/9	K/9	K	GB%	BABIP
2019	WSX	ROK	18	0	0	0	3	3	3	2	0	6.0	6.0	2	33.3%	.222
2021 FS	CHW	MLB	20	2	3	0	57	0	50	50	8	5.6	7.2	39	37.5%	.284

Comparables: Juan Minaya, Elvis Luciano, José Torres

There are many younger players in professional baseball, but few are younger-looking than Dalquist. The six-foot-one, 20-year-old wood sprite commands three pitches and has the athleticism and projection to imagine him working in a major league rotation in three years, at which time he could accrue enough facial hair to look 15 years of age.

Chicago White Sox 2021

YEAR	TEAM	LVL	AGE	WHIP	ERA	DRA-	WARP	MPH	FB%	WHF	CSP
2019	WSX	ROK	18	1.33	0.00						
2021 FS	CHW	MLB	20	1.62	5.65	125	-0.5				

Odrisamer Despaigne   RHP
Born: 04/04/87   Age: 34   Bats: R   Throws: R
Height: 6'0"   Weight: 200   Origin: International Free Agent, 2014

YEAR	TEAM	LVL	AGE	W	L	SV	G	GS	IP	H	HR	BB/9	K/9	K	GB%	BABIP
2018	NO	AAA	31	2	3	2	13	4	43^1	52	0	2.5	8.3	40	43.1%	.380
2018	LAA	MLB	31	0	3	0	8	4	18^2	30	3	5.3	8.2	17	44.1%	.415
2018	MIA	MLB	31	2	0	0	11	1	20^1	22	1	3.5	8.0	18	39.1%	.339
2019	CHA	AAA	32	5	4	0	16	14	83	83	6	3.0	9.1	84	47.7%	.335
2019	LOU	AAA	32	3	2	0	8	8	41^1	40	5	3.5	8.7	40	50.8%	.310
2019	CHW	MLB	32	0	2	0	3	3	13^1	24	3	4.7	4.7	7	28.3%	.420
2020	KT	KBO	33	15	8	0	35	34	207^2	233	18	2.0	6.6	152		
2021 FS	CHW	MLB	34	2	3	0	57	0	50	51	8	3.8	7.6	42	42.6%	.294

Comparables: Trevor Cahill, Ross Ohlendorf, Josh A. Smith

At a glance, Despaigne's numbers aren't all that impressive, and the two statistics that best capture his importance to KT—games started and innings pitched—are usually afterthoughts. But unlike in MLB, where the third time through the order penalty reduces a team's incentive to push their starters, top arms in the KBO need to eat innings. Usually, they do so as part of a six-day rotation, as every Monday is an off-day in the KBO. KT took a different tack with Despaigne, using him on a five-day schedule all season long. Working with less rest than anybody else, the journeyman right-hander still posted a well-above average ERA and FIP, all while making five more starts and tossing 50 more innings than the typical foreign signing. Those extra starts and innings would have otherwise gone to one of three longmen, all of whom notched ERAs on the wrong side of six. In a year where KT snuck into second place, a single game ahead of fifth-place Kiwoom, two things are clear: Manager Lee Kang-chul deserves a tip of the cap, and Despaigne deserves a raise.

YEAR	TEAM	LVL	AGE	WHIP	ERA	DRA-	WARP	MPH	FB%	WHF	CSP
2018	NO	AAA	31	1.48	4.36	82	0.7				
2018	LAA	MLB	31	2.20	8.20	150	-0.4	95.0	67.2%	20.9%	
2018	MIA	MLB	31	1.48	5.31	103	0.1	94.1	71.6%	31.3%	
2019	CHA	AAA	32	1.34	3.25	90	1.8				
2019	LOU	AAA	32	1.35	3.92	105	0.6				
2019	CHW	MLB	32	2.33	9.45	205	-0.6	94.5	74.8%	13.6%	
2020	KT	KBO	33	1.45	4.33						
2021 FS	CHW	MLB	34	1.44	4.88	109	0.0	94.6	71.5%	20.9%	45.9%

Bernardo Flores Jr. LHP

Born: 08/23/95   Age: 25   Bats: L   Throws: L
Height: 6'4"   Weight: 190   Origin: Round 7, 2016 Draft (#206 overall)

YEAR	TEAM	LVL	AGE	W	L	SV	G	GS	IP	H	HR	BB/9	K/9	K	GB%	BABIP
2018	WS	HI-A	22	5	4	0	12	12	77^2	75	5	2.0	6.7	58	52.7%	.298
2018	BIR	AA	22	3	5	0	13	13	78^1	79	5	1.6	5.4	47	47.8%	.306
2019	WSX	ROK	23	0	0	0	4	4	12	17	2	0.8	9.8	13	54.3%	.455
2019	KAN	LO-A	23	0	0	0	1	1	3	6	0	3.0	0.0	0	69.2%	.462
2019	BIR	AA	23	3	8	0	15	15	78^1	74	10	1.7	7.9	69	53.6%	.284
2020	CHW	MLB	24	0	0	0	2	0	2	4	0	0.0	9.0	2	62.5%	.500
2021 FS	CHW	MLB	25	2	2	0	57	0	50	50	7	2.7	6.9	38	49.3%	.289
2021 DC	CHW	MLB	25	1	1	0	31	0	22.3	22	3	2.7	6.9	17	49.3%	.289

Comparables: Ryan Helsley, Robert Dugger, Jorge Alcala

In both High-A and Double-A, Flores' predilection for racking up groundball outs with yeoman-like repetition earned him the nickname Mr. Quality Start. In the wacky world of projecting pitchers, this most likely ends in him never getting them, instead scrapping his way toward pitching one or two innings of mid-leverage relief. Flores relieved in college, so officially nothing about this path makes sense other than to say that this is baseball.

YEAR	TEAM	LVL	AGE	WHIP	ERA	DRA-	WARP	MPH	FB%	WHF	CSP
2018	WS	HI-A	22	1.18	2.55	72	1.8				
2018	BIR	AA	22	1.19	2.76	85	1.2				
2019	WSX	ROK	23	1.50	3.75						
2019	KAN	LO-A	23	2.33	9.00	174	-0.1				
2019	BIR	AA	23	1.14	3.33	90	0.5				
2020	CHW	MLB	24	2.00	9.00	85	0.0	93.5	59.3%	20.0%	
2021 FS	CHW	MLB	25	1.31	4.08	96	0.3	93.5	59.3%	20.0%	58.8%
2021 DC	CHW	MLB	25	1.31	4.08	96	0.2	93.5	59.3%	20.0%	58.8%

Jared Kelley RHP

Born: 10/03/01   Age: 19   Bats: R   Throws: R
Height: 6'3"   Weight: 215   Origin: Round 2, 2020 Draft (#47 overall)

The comparisons to large animals known for dragging heavy payloads come fast and furious when Kelley's name comes up. For the horse and/or ox-like 19-year-old, the only thing about him that looks its age is his lack of a statistical record, as he transitioned after the draft from cooking overmatched Houston-area high schoolers for all of 12 innings in his senior year, to being overmatched against Quad-A hitters in uncounted sim games in Schaumburg.

Chicago White Sox 2021

Michael Kopech   RHP

Born: 04/30/96   Age: 25   Bats: R   Throws: R
Height: 6'3"   Weight: 225   Origin: Round 1, 2014 Draft (#33 overall)

YEAR	TEAM	LVL	AGE	W	L	SV	G	GS	IP	H	HR	BB/9	K/9	K	GB%	BABIP
2018	CHA	AAA	22	7	7	0	24	24	126^1	101	9	4.3	12.1	170	38.7%	.319
2018	CHW	MLB	22	1	1	0	4	4	14^1	20	4	1.3	9.4	15	28.3%	.381
2021 FS	CHW	MLB	25	9	9	0	26	26	150	131	21	5.2	10.5	174	37.2%	.293
2021 DC	CHW	MLB	25	5	5	0	19	19	89.3	78	12	5.2	10.5	103	37.2%	.293

Comparables: Trevor Bauer, Henry Owens, Matt Wisler

    Contrary to popular belief, Michael Kopech did actually pitch in 2020. It came in March, in the absolute last spring training game the White Sox played before COVID-19 shut down the American sports world for months on end. Pulsing with adrenaline in something closer to his actual "real" return to the mound from Tommy John surgery than a few outings in 2019 instructional league, Kopech hit 100 mph with his first fastball, then hit 101 mph, and within 11 pitches, his perfect single inning of work was over. He was still buzzing a half hour later when he spoke to reports; outdoors, with all of them standing six feet away. He was too jacked up to remember when he was scheduled to pitch next.

    "I assume it's in five days," he said.

    In fairness, Kopech's assumption performed about as well as everyone else's in the post-pandemic world. When the White Sox next contacted Kopech about pitching in 2020, it came with the weight of uncertainty about virus testing, safety, proper ramp-up time for a season, sacrificing contact with family, and a host of other uncertainties, and Kopech decided not to take part. That judgment, equally of its time, figures to age better.

YEAR	TEAM	LVL	AGE	WHIP	ERA	DRA-	WARP	MPH	FB%	WHF	CSP
2018	CHA	AAA	22	1.27	3.70	105	0.5				
2018	CHW	MLB	22	1.53	5.02	152	-0.3	97.6	62.5%	21.5%	
2021 FS	CHW	MLB	25	1.45	4.64	104	1.1	97.6	62.5%	21.5%	51.0%
2021 DC	CHW	MLB	25	1.45	4.64	104	0.7	97.6	62.5%	21.5%	51.0%

Jimmy Lambert   RHP

Born: 11/18/94   Age: 26   Bats: R   Throws: R
Height: 6'2"   Weight: 190   Origin: Round 5, 2016 Draft (#146 overall)

YEAR	TEAM	LVL	AGE	W	L	SV	G	GS	IP	H	HR	BB/9	K/9	K	GB%	BABIP
2018	WS	HI-A	23	5	7	0	13	13	70^2	57	5	2.7	10.2	80	39.9%	.301
2018	BIR	AA	23	3	1	0	5	5	25	20	2	2.2	10.8	30	40.0%	.286
2019	BIR	AA	24	3	4	0	11	11	59^1	62	11	4.1	10.6	70	37.0%	.338
2020	CHW	MLB	25	0	0	0	2	0	2	2	0	0.0	9.0	2	33.3%	.333
2021 FS	CHW	MLB	26	2	2	0	57	0	50	47	8	3.7	8.7	48	36.7%	.287
2021 DC	CHW	MLB	26	2	1	0	13	3	31.3	30	5	3.7	8.7	30	36.7%	.287

Comparables: Sterling Sharp, Patrick Murphy, Brandon Woodruff

In another world, it's Lambert, not Dane Dunning, who is nominally starting Chicago's decidedly cursed Game 3 playoff loss in Oakland. The White Sox tabbed Lambert for their Opening Day roster because they felt he was ahead of the former first rounder at the time. Despite sitting at similar lower-90s velocities, Lambert is more at home throwing like a power pitcher. He gets convincing ride at the top of the zone with his four-seamer and has a curveball and changeup that work off of it well. The rub is that Lambert might have only been sitting at Dunning-like velocities because his surgically repaired elbow was already barking. Now instead of the seemingly standard issue rite of passage of Tommy John surgery, his path appears more like two full years of arm troubles with fits of activity sprinkled in. Lambert has the arsenal to start, but two relief appearances mixed amid injury present a worst-case scenario for his future.

YEAR	TEAM	LVL	AGE	WHIP	ERA	DRA-	WARP	MPH	FB%	WHF	CSP
2018	WS	HI-A	23	1.10	3.95	67	1.8				
2018	BIR	AA	23	1.04	2.88	56	0.8				
2019	BIR	AA	24	1.50	4.55	114	-0.4				
2020	CHW	MLB	25	1.00	0.00	100	0.0	96.3	48.5%	28.6%	
2021 FS	CHW	MLB	26	1.36	4.44	103	0.2	96.3	48.5%	28.6%	53.3%
2021 DC	CHW	MLB	26	1.36	4.44	103	0.1	96.3	48.5%	28.6%	53.3%

Carlos Rodón LHP

Born: 12/10/92   Age: 28   Bats: L   Throws: L
Height: 6'3"   Weight: 250   Origin: Round 1, 2014 Draft (#3 overall)

YEAR	TEAM	LVL	AGE	W	L	SV	G	GS	IP	H	HR	BB/9	K/9	K	GB%	BABIP
2018	CHA	AAA	25	1	0	0	3	3	12²	10	0	3.6	15.6	22	56.5%	.435
2018	CHW	MLB	25	6	8	0	20	20	120²	97	15	4.1	6.7	90	41.6%	.243
2019	CHW	MLB	26	3	2	0	7	7	34²	33	4	4.4	11.9	46	41.5%	.322
2020	CHW	MLB	27	0	2	0	4	2	7²	9	1	3.5	7.0	6	28.0%	.333
2021 FS	CHW	MLB	28	9	9	0	26	26	150	138	23	4.7	9.7	161	40.0%	.293
2021 DC	CHW	MLB	28	6	6	0	44	12	82.3	76	13	4.7	9.7	88	40.0%	.293

Comparables: Daniel Mengden, Daniel Norris, Zach Davies

There's a crowd, a seemingly growing one, that has responded to the waves of pitching injuries and resulting surgeries with a mixture of patience and resignation. "Just get the surgery!" they howl, annoyed with how all the efforts to rehab and forestall such a leap seemingly stall the end date where injuries can be forgotten about forever. But there is no surgery that can deliver that final erasure of physical trauma. It all adds up and compiles, and even the found footholds are known to be temporary. Four years removed from a promising sophomore campaign that served as portent for his best years in the majors, Rodón is still looking for a spot to rest his feet where the ground will not give way beneath. There have been incisions made to his incisions made into his shoulder and elbow over the past three years. At times, in 2020, the mid-90s velocity flickered into being, just long enough to cast a shadow. But the residue of it all still hangs over him. There is no surgery that can recreate the Rodón of 2016, just an exploratory one to discover what remains of him in 2021.

YEAR	TEAM	LVL	AGE	WHIP	ERA	DRA-	WARP	MPH	FB%	WHF	CSP
2018	CHA	AAA	25	1.18	1.42	67	0.3				
2018	CHW	MLB	25	1.26	4.18	146	-1.8	95.8	59.8%	21.3%	
2019	CHW	MLB	26	1.44	5.19	83	0.6	94.1	51.9%	28.5%	
2020	CHW	MLB	27	1.57	8.22	151	-0.1	96.7	51.1%	23.3%	
2021 FS	CHW	MLB	28	1.44	4.68	104	1.1	95.3	55.9%	24.2%	47.4%
2021 DC	CHW	MLB	28	1.44	4.68	104	0.5	95.3	55.9%	24.2%	47.4%

Jonathan Stiever RHP

Born: 05/12/97   Age: 24   Bats: R   Throws: R
Height: 6'2"   Weight: 215   Origin: Round 5, 2018 Draft (#138 overall)

YEAR	TEAM	LVL	AGE	W	L	SV	G	GS	IP	H	HR	BB/9	K/9	K	GB%	BABIP
2018	GTF	ROK	21	0	1	0	13	13	28	23	3	2.9	12.5	39	47.7%	.323
2019	KAN	LO-A	22	4	6	0	14	14	74	88	10	1.7	9.4	77	43.8%	.363
2019	WS	HI-A	22	6	4	0	12	12	71	56	7	1.6	9.8	77	40.4%	.278
2020	CHW	MLB	23	0	1	0	2	2	6¹	7	4	5.7	4.3	3	40.9%	.167
2021 FS	CHW	MLB	24	2	2	0	57	0	50	49	8	3.3	7.8	43	40.4%	.287
2021 DC	CHW	MLB	24	2	2	0	25	6	28.3	28	4	3.3	7.8	24	40.4%	.287

Comparables: Beau Burrows, Felix Jorge, Andrew Heaney

As of March 2020, Stiever found himself in the Carolina League, sidelined by forearm soreness; that he ended the season with major league experience makes it hard to spin his year as a negative. Stopping short of that, it's fairer to be confused about where he stands. The results—one suitable outing against a moribund offense, one night of getting absolutely tattooed—fit alongside his place on the developmental track. But since he achieved them lacking the power stuff, velocity and swing-and-miss results that defined his ascent to prospect status, it was a dispiriting coda to a year that began with an injury scare. Stiever is an exceptional athlete with the ability to spin it. He seemed to gain some feel for a changeup even as his mid-90s heat took a break, and those raw ingredients will spur optimism going forward. But if the takeaway from 2020 for most prospects is confusion over how to assess how much they progressed without minor league action, Stiever's major league turn did not pump more certainty into the information gap.

YEAR	TEAM	LVL	AGE	WHIP	ERA	DRA-	WARP	MPH	FB%	WHF	CSP
2018	GTF	ROK	21	1.14	4.18						
2019	KAN	LO-A	22	1.38	4.74	123	-0.7				
2019	WS	HI-A	22	0.97	2.15	64	1.7				
2020	CHW	MLB	23	1.74	9.95	148	-0.1	94.2	53.3%	14.5%	
2021 FS	CHW	MLB	24	1.36	4.51	105	0.1	94.2	53.3%	14.5%	48.4%
2021 DC	CHW	MLB	24	1.36	4.51	105	0.2	94.2	53.3%	14.5%	48.4%

Chicago White Sox 2021

Matthew Thompson RHP

Born: 08/11/00   Age: 20   Bats: R   Throws: R
Height: 6'3"   Weight: 195   Origin: Round 2, 2019 Draft (#45 overall)

YEAR	TEAM	LVL	AGE	W	L	SV	G	GS	IP	H	HR	BB/9	K/9	K	GB%	BABIP
2019	WSX	ROK	18	0	0	0	2	2	2	2	0	0.0	9.0	2	33.3%	.333
2021 FS	CHW	MLB	20	2	3	0	57	0	50	50	8	5.4	7.4	41	38.2%	.287

Comparables: Nick Adenhart, Will Smith, Elvis Luciano

The best photos of Thompson in action still find him in a Cypress Ranch High School uniform. Updates about his progress on backfields and alternate sites are light on descriptions of actual innings pitched, and center around if he's figured out how to throw a changeup. Yet his build, athleticism and burgeoning command all point to someone who could grow into a rotation role, assuming minor league baseball ever comes back and he actually gets to pitch.

YEAR	TEAM	LVL	AGE	WHIP	ERA	DRA-	WARP	MPH	FB%	WHF	CSP
2019	WSX	ROK	18	1.00	0.00						
2021 FS	CHW	MLB	20	1.60	5.54	123	-0.4				

Emilio Vargas RHP

Born: 08/12/96   Age: 24   Bats: R   Throws: R
Height: 6'3"   Weight: 230   Origin: International Free Agent, 2013

YEAR	TEAM	LVL	AGE	W	L	SV	G	GS	IP	H	HR	BB/9	K/9	K	GB%	BABIP
2018	VIS	HI-A	21	8	5	0	20	19	108	92	7	3.4	11.7	140	39.3%	.335
2018	JXN	AA	21	1	3	0	6	6	35^2	31	6	2.0	7.6	30	42.2%	.245
2019	DIA	ROK	22	0	2	0	3	3	10^1	9	1	1.7	10.5	12	32.0%	.333
2019	JXN	AA	22	5	3	0	17	17	85^2	74	10	2.4	7.4	70	43.1%	.261
2021 FS	CHW	MLB	24	2	3	0	57	0	50	48	8	4.0	8.1	45	40.9%	.282

Comparables: Pedro Avila, Anthony Swarzak, Brady Lail

The Diamondbacks have a thing for guys with vertical arm slots and Emilio Vargas fits that mold. Maybe the White Sox do too, since they claimed him off waivers in November. He seems likely to see some big-league time if he can survive the winter on the 40-man roster.

YEAR	TEAM	LVL	AGE	WHIP	ERA	DRA-	WARP	MPH	FB%	WHF	CSP
2018	VIS	HI-A	21	1.23	2.50	80	1.7				
2018	JXN	AA	21	1.09	4.04	80	0.6				
2019	DIA	ROK	22	1.06	4.35						
2019	JXN	AA	22	1.13	3.78	92	0.5				
2021 FS	CHW	MLB	24	1.41	4.75	109	0.0				

White Sox Prospects

The State of the System:
It's a good thing the White Sox have one of the best and most dynamic lineups in baseball, because this is a very pitching heavy system now.

The Top Ten:

★ ★ ★ *2021 Top 101 Prospect* **#12** ★ ★ ★

1
Nick Madrigal 2B   OFP: 60   ETA: Debuted in 2020
Born: 03/05/97   Age: 24   Bats: R   Throws: R   Height: 5'8"   Weight: 175
Origin: Round 1, 2018 Draft (#4 overall)

The Report: How good of a baseball player can you be in the 2020s if you don't hit the ball hard in the air? Madrigal has some of the best contact abilities in the game. He has an elite hit tool, potentially an 80. He's an excellent defensive second baseman, probably skilled enough to play on the other side of the keystone if needed. He runs well. He has more raw power than you'd think given his 20 game power, probably 40 or 45 on balance, and he actually had a 112-mph batted ball in the majors.

In an age where launch angle optimization and exit velocity have become king, Madrigal hits the ball on the ground a whole lot and, on average, not particularly hard. He did not have a single "barrel" as defined by Statcast this year. While there's still the potential for him to at least occasionally start driving the ball in the air, he didn't do it at all in the majors, and that's an upper-bound limitation on his profile unless he actually does hit .340 every year. He's going to single his way into being an awfully good player anyways, but we were already pretty confident of that outcome, and we're less optimistic that gap game power is coming than we were a year ago.

Development Track: Madrigal remains unexpectedly eligible for this list because of a separated shoulder that cost him three-and-a-half weeks around the middle of the season. He had surgery after the season, and he might not be ready for spring training. His slash line was extreme even for his current skill set, owing to a .365 BABIP and a .029 ISO. We'd expect the former to go a bit down and the latter to go a bit up over the longer term even without future adjustments. As ridiculous as this sounds, he might have a little more room for growth in his contact rate, which was "only" 91.2 percent, fourth in the majors for players with 100 or more plate appearances.

Variance: Low, subject to his shoulder not being a long-term concern. If we were still doing our old OFP/likely outcome spread, I'd probably argue for a 60/60 here.

J.P. Breen's Fantasy Take: Some fantasy experts remain skeptical of Madrigal's path to fantasy relevance, but he's a potential #categorycarrier in two troublesome categories: batting average and stolen bases. Madrigal could offer a .300-plus average with 20-plus stolen bases and a boatload of runs. Power is easy to find these days, but average-and-speed guys are not. Madrigal's skill set projects to be incredibly useful—think early-career Jose Altuve, before the power spike.

─────── ★ ★ ★ *2021 Top 101 Prospect* **#14** ★ ★ ★ ───────

2 Andrew Vaughn 1B   OFP: 60   ETA: Early 2021
Born: 04/03/98   Age: 23   Bats: R   Throws: R   Height: 6'0"   Weight: 215
Origin: Round 1, 2019 Draft (#3 overall)

The Report: Until Spencer Torkelson came around a year later, Vaughn was the highest-drafted college first baseman since the 1990s. (We'll ignore Detroit's suggestion for a moment that Torkelson might really be a third baseman.) Given the industry preference against taking right-handed bat-only players in the top five of the draft, you'd expect Vaughn to be an elite hitting prospect even if you knew absolutely nothing else about him. We're looking at a plus hit tool and plus power, with both of those being light if anything, and one of the best plate approaches of any prospect in the minors. He's a first baseman, occasional fantastical notions about trying third or the outfield aside, so he's going to have to *hit*. And he should.

Development Track: This is one of the reports where we just don't have a lot of fantastically interesting stuff to say about Vaughn's 2020. We got consistently strong reports on his bat from the alternate site at Schaumburg, although he didn't force himself to the majors immediately either. Everything seems perfectly on track, and the White Sox look likely to have plenty of 1B/DH playing time available as soon as he's ready.

Variance: Low. We're pretty confident in this bat.

J.P. Breen's Fantasy Take: Despite posting pedestrian numbers in his professional debut in 2019, Vaughn remains a top-10 dynasty prospect and a top-100 overall dynasty player. He is a potential four-category monster—whether in AVG or OBP leagues—and he should make his big-league debut in 2021. The fact that the White Sox project to be an offensive powerhouse obviously increases his short-term value, but given his glowing scouting reports, Vaughn should be a long-term fantasy stalwart for the foreseeable future. Grab him where you can.

★ ★ ★ *2021 Top 101 Prospect* **#36** ★ ★ ★

3

Garrett Crochet   LHP   OFP: 60   ETA: Debuted in 2020
Born: 06/21/99   Age: 22   Bats: L   Throws: L   Height: 6'6"   Weight: 218
Origin: Round 1, 2020 Draft (#11 overall)

The Report: In what amounted to a very short amateur track record, Crochet's flashes of dominance could not be overlooked. Starting in only a third of his appearances in college, including just one instance of game action in the spring, the tall, lefty fireballer simply had too much upside to pass up with the 11th-overall pick. Reports last fall indicated his fastball had gained an extra gear up from its already plus velocity, adding some snap to the slider as well. Even the changeup was coming along. With all the arrows trending upward on his projectable frame and present big-league stuff, it was only a minor surprise to see him force his way onto the bullpen late in the season and playoff run. The huge velocity seen in shorter stints is likely to head back into the mid-90s range as he returns to a starter role moving forward and until further notice.

Development Track: With the velo spike came some barking arm troubles, which again flared up in what became the final game of the White Sox season. The amount of power he generates from a short arm action on a lower slot could make starting over a long period of time unmanageable. If that is in fact the case, we all saw just how dominating he was in the late innings. The heater/slider combo is good enough to erase any platoon advantage, however, the increased development of the changeup will help further his case as a future starter beyond any health concerns.

Variance: High. The small sample size is both promising and worrisome.

J.P. Breen's Fantasy Take: With the number of pop-up pitching prospects that annually emerge, as well as the increased value of middle-relief arms in fantasy, Crochet is the type of arm that I value much more highly than most fantasy analysts. If the lefty makes it as a starter or a reliever, he's elite in either role. We're talking an SP2, at least, or an elite closer in the Josh Hader mold. His health remains a gargantuan question mark, but that's always true to some extent with pitching prospects. If I'm going to take up a minor-league roster spot with a pitcher, Crochet is precisely the pitching profile I want to target: the potential fantasy monster. I ain't running a real-life fantasy team after all.

★ ★ ★ *2021 Top 101 Prospect* **#37** ★ ★ ★

4

Michael Kopech   RHP   OFP: 60   ETA: Debuted in 2018
Born: 04/30/96   Age: 25   Bats: R   Throws: R   Height: 6'3"   Weight: 225
Origin: Round 1, 2014 Draft (#33 overall)

The Report: It's unusual that we would still be ranking a prospect who debuted in 2018 on our 2021 lists. When it does happen you can usually assume it's a pitcher and Tommy John surgery was involved. Kopech played to the scouting report in his four 2018 outings, mid-90s, high spin heat that touched higher, and a power slider that missed bats. The control gains he showed in the minors continued, at least in those few MLB appearances. He didn't get the chance to convince us he was a starter long term before he tore his UCL, but the stuff will play in any role.

Development Track: Kopech chose not to play in the 2020 season. Besides the completely reasonable concerns about playing in a global pandemic, Kopech was still recovering from Tommy John surgery and would have had a short ramp up. Now he gets a normal offseason and hopefully more normal spring training. For our purposes though, it does limit the information we have about his present stuff. We've chosen to not consider the additional missed year off Tommy John as we really just don't know more than we knew a year ago.

Variance: High. Kopech was major-league-ready pre-surgery, but hasn't thrown a competitive pitch since September 2018.

J.P. Breen's Fantasy Take: Kopech is overrated in re-draft formats and underrated in dynasty circles. The right-hander has too many short-term question marks to be selected in front of guys like Marcus Stroman and James Paxton, which has been true according to early NFBC numbers, but has too much long-term talent to be ranked 100-plus spots behind someone like Nate Pearson on dynasty lists. Kopech has a high-octane fastball-slider combination that misses plenty of bats, and he had shown improvement in his command in the upper minors and the majors before his injury. The problem: The right-hander is coming off Tommy John surgery and hasn't pitched since 2018. Then again, to use someone like Pearson as a comparison, Pearson missed time in 2020 with elbow issues and isn't much less of an injury risk. Kopech is a potential SP2, though he shouldn't be treated as such for those only interested in fantasy production in 2021.

5   **Jared Kelley**   **RHP**   OFP: 55   ETA: 2024
Born: 10/03/01   Age: 19   Bats: R   Throws: R   Height: 6'3"   Weight: 215
Origin: Round 2, 2020 Draft (#47 overall)

The Report: As the 2020 draft cycle came into focus, Kelley was in a tight race for the top prep arm in the class and a possible top 10 pick. Unlike many high school players, the early spring season for Texas allowed for further scrutiny that caused many evaluators to soften their opinion. The fastball that was in the mid-to-upper 90s and topping near 100 during the previous summer showcase months dropped a tick and questions about his husky body dropped his stock heading into draft day. One scout referred to him as, "Tyler Kolek with a changeup," which you can interpret however you wish. On the plus side, there were plenty of positive reviews in camp upon signing, signaling the potential steal of a first-round talent in the second.

Development Track: The fastball and changeup, including the command of both pitches, are advanced for his age. What is clearly needed as he transitions to a professional training program is work on his slurvy breaking ball and tightening up the overall physique. That's a pretty solid foundation for a player who was picked apart—perhaps both by sample and recency bias—prior to the draft.

Variance: Extreme. High school pitchers are notoriously risky, especially the strong-armed kind. Enough question marks exist several years down the road to gauge this sort of risk.

J.P. Breen's Fantasy Take: We're now six prospects into this list, and I've officially tapped out. This ain't my bag. Kelley is your prototypical hard-throwing righty about whom we'll know nothing significant for a year or two. If you're in a deep dynasty league, he's worth a dart throw if you love hard-throwing prep arms—the advanced changeup makes him more interesting than most—but I wouldn't advise investing more than a late-round pick in offseason supplemental drafts. You'll be able to find similar arms on the waiver wire or in next year's draft class with little trouble.

6. Jonathan Stiever   RHP   OFP: 55   ETA: Debuted in 2020

Born: 05/12/97   Age: 24   Bats: R   Throws: R   Height: 6'2"   Weight: 215
Origin: Round 5, 2018 Draft (#138 overall)

The Report: The summer of 2019 saw Stiever go from cold weather fifth-rounder to hot prospect with helium thanks to 71 dominant innings at High-A Winston-Salem. In the Carolina League he showcased a mid-90s fastball and two above-average breaking pitches. Stiever wasn't the perfect starting pitching prospect but he was promising; control over command but with very good control, not racking up all that many strikeouts yet exhibiting swing-and-miss stuff. He's also a good athlete with a repeatable delivery that bodes well for future command gains.

Development Track: There were a couple of concerning trends that cropped up in Stiever's 2020, a season that began with a forearm injury scare and ended with a rocky introduction to the big leagues. The devastating fastball/breaking ball combo that impressed us in 2019 wasn't there when he made his major league debut. The riding fastball that was sitting 94-96 is now running at 92-94, and neither the slider nor the curveball seem to have the bite that they used to. The slider in particular lacks the sharp downward movement that used to distinguish it, and with it most of its swing-and-miss quality. A more encouraging sign is his increasingly viable changeup that would round out a starter's repertoire.

Variance: Medium. The stuff backed up in 2020 but it was an anomalous season in which he was hampered by injury, and it will be interesting to see if it bounces back next spring.

J.P. Breen's Fantasy Take: Stiever's brief cup o' coffee in 2020 was disastrous, but don't hold that against him. The 23-year-old had never thrown a professional inning above High-A before being rocketed to the big leagues, where he had home-run issues, command issues, and bat-missing issues. That performance will ensure that he's available in almost all dynasty formats, either on the waiver wire or via trade, but he's still a potential SP5 who saw his stuff take a step backward in 2020. If your league rosters approximately 250 prospects, he's worth a stash. Dynasty owners in shallower leagues can feel free to move on without a tinge of hesitation.

7. Andrew Dalquist   RHP   OFP: 50   ETA: 2024
Born: 11/13/00   Age: 20   Bats: R   Throws: R   Height: 6'1"   Weight: 175
Origin: Round 3, 2019 Draft (#81 overall)

The Report: The White Sox took Dalquist as an over-slot prep righty in the third round of the 2019 draft. He was an advanced arm at the time, flashing above-average velocity and working a full four-pitch mix, unusual for even a seven-figure prep.

Development Track: We paired Dalquist with Matthew Thompson on last year's list coming off the 2019 draft, but this year's instructs reports have the California righty showing a more complete arsenal led by a fastball that bumped 96. The curve is the most advanced secondary, but it's a quality overall repertoire, and Dalquist has a better chance to start long term despite lacking Thompson's prototypical size.

Variance: High. There's already four pitches with at least average potential, but Dalquist doesn't have much physical projection or pro experience and is a long ways off from pitching on the South Side.

J.P. Breen's Fantasy Take: A semi-projectable prep righty who is a potential No. 4 starter and had a bit of a velocity bump in instructs? When will one of those ever come around again?! Dalquist is an interesting real-life prospect who has a legit pathway to a useful big-league role in four or five years. For dynasty, the right-hander is just one of a few-dozen projectable teenage arms who could be irrelevant by August. Don't bother for now.

8. Codi Heuer   RHP   OFP: 50   ETA: Debuted in 2020
Born: 07/03/96   Age: 25   Bats: R   Throws: R   Height: 6'5"   Weight: 190
Origin: Round 6, 2018 Draft (#168 overall)

The Report: Heuer went from nondescript starting prospect to high-leverage big league reliever in two seasons thanks to his nasty sinker and deceptive sidearm delivery. His slider flashes plus and is a useful swing-and-miss pitch against both righties and lefties, and he's fared well against both despite initially profiling as more of a right-on-right specialist. His changeup is also viable, if seldom used. Heuer's top-line numbers outpaced his peripherals in his first big league campaign, but even if he regresses a bit he should still be a key cog in the White Sox 'pen for the near term.

Development Track: It's possible he's just about reached his final form, but Heuer could rise on the bullpen depth chart if he refines his command and works to get more consistent results with his secondaries.

Variance: Low. He was a reliable arm out of the 'pen last season and there's nothing indicating that this should be a fluke.

J.P. Breen's Fantasy Take: Our own Mike Gianella has been highlighting the unheralded value of big-league middle relievers in recent weeks. Heuer is worth tracking, as he posted a 14.4 percent swinging-strike rate and gets tons of groundballs. His BABIP should rise going forward, obviously, but we're still talking about a potential late-inning reliever who strikes out more than a batter per inning with decent rates. He needs to refine his command; however, Heuer is closer to fantasy relevance than the previous three prospects. Just remember that Heuer is a potential waiver-wire grab, not someone to target in drafts. There are too many Heuers in Major League Baseball these days to waste draft picks on him.

9 Jimmy Lambert RHP OFP: 50 ETA: Debuted in 2020
Born: 11/18/94 Age: 26 Bats: R Throws: R Height: 6'2" Weight: 190
Origin: Round 5, 2016 Draft (#146 overall)

The Report / Development Track: Lambert was closing in on the majors when he had Tommy John surgery in summer 2019. We were a bit surprised to see him show back up in the majors to start 2020; in last offseason's list we predicted he'd miss most or all of the season. He threw in two games in July and promptly missed the rest of the season with a flexor strain, which is often related to UCL problems. He's got swing-and-miss stuff, four pitches that can come in at average-to-above from a deceptively high arm slot. The flip side is that he just turned 26 and hasn't even come close to establishing himself as a big-league starter yet. We think he can be an effective MLB pitcher in 2021, we're just not sure in what role he'll hold up in.

Variance: High. On the one hand, he's major-league-ready. On the other hand, he's had Tommy John and a subsequent elbow issue.

J.P. Breen's Fantasy Take: A potential back-end starter who has a history of elbow problems and maybe an elbow problem right now. He'll be on the waiver wire in your dynasty league. If you need pitching, grab him off waivers if he's healthy and in the majors in 2021. Otherwise, don't bother.

10 Matthew Thompson RHP OFP: 50 ETA: 2024
Born: 08/11/00 Age: 20 Bats: R Throws: R Height: 6'3" Weight: 195
Origin: Round 2, 2019 Draft (#45 overall)

The Report / Development Track: We paired Thompson and Dalquist on last year's list, and while the latter has moved ahead in 2020, Thompson is a good pitching prospect in his own right, although there were concerns about how much more physicality he will add to his frame, and his fastball velocity was a couple ticks behind Dalquist in the complex. The breaking ball has improved enough that there's a useful reliever role fallback now. As I wrote last year, the story on those two prep arms is far from finished. Check back again next year after both have spent time in full-season ball.

Variance: High. It's a relatively advanced breaking ball, but Thompson hasn't advanced through the minors much

J.P. Breen's Fantasy Take: Thompson can be categorized with the other highly volatile prep pitchers ... except his velocity already fluctuates a ton. More has to go right here than with most high-school hurlers, which means he's not a top-400 dynasty prospect.

The Prospects You Meet Outside The Top Ten:

Safe MLB bats, but less upside than you'd like

Blake Rutherford RF Born: 05/02/97 Age: 24 Bats: L Throws: R Height: 6'3" Weight: 210 Origin: Round 1, 2016 Draft (#18 overall)

Rutherford remains tied in my mind to a different org's center fielder. He and Mickey Moniak were both sure-shot bats among the prep outfield class of 2016. Rutherford didn't have the albatross of "first overall pick" hanging over his development track, but like Moniak he's never really hit as much as the amateur reports prophesied. There were suggestions of some power improvements at the alternate site this year, but like Moniak he might end up "just" a bench outfielder.

Personal Cheeseball, sort of

Jake Burger 3B Born: 04/10/96 Age: 25 Bats: R Throws: R Height: 6'2" Weight: 210 Origin: Round 1, 2017 Draft (#11 overall)

Burger finally made it back on the field after two Achilles tears wiped out his 2018 and 2019 seasons. He spent some time in the CarShield Collegiate Summer League, the alternate site in Schaumberg, and White Sox instructs. Third base isn't really an option anymore, but the plus-plus bat speed and power are still present. It would be a great story if he can make it to the majors, and we aren't gonna bet against the bat even now.

Some upside, but a ways away

Bryan Ramos 3B Born: 03/12/02 Age: 19 Bats: R Throws: R Height: 6'2" Weight: 190 Origin: International Free Agent, 2018

The White Sox no longer have a system overflowing with high-upside, high-dollar IFAs, but Ramos—signed for $300k in 2018—can really hit. He'll need to given the corner profile, but the bat stood out in Camelback.

Top Talents 25 and Under (as of 4/1/2021):

1. Yoán Moncada, 3B
2. Eloy Jiménez, OF
3. Luis Robert, OF
4. Nick Madrigal, 2B
5. Andrew Vaughn, 1B
6. Garrett Crochet, LHP
7. Michael Kopech, RHP
8. Dane Dunning, RHP
9. Dylan Cease, RHP
10. Jared Kelley, RHP

The White Sox have three recently-graduated global top 10 prospects, so this is a pretty loaded 25-and-under list. Yoán Moncada topped this list last year, and tops it again this year. At points during and after the season Moncada mentioned battling long-term health issues stemming from a summer bout with COVID-19; given that, talking about his on-field performance seems trite and irrelevant. One only has to go back to 2019 to see a sensational campaign from our 2017 No. 5 prospect, and we hope he'll get back to that moving forward.

Of the recent White Sox list graduates, Eloy Jiménez's development has been the most linear in the majors. Our 2019 No. 4 prospect showed up in 2019 after signing a pre-debut arbitration buyout and was more or less immediately the player we expected him to be: a plus hitter who is getting to nearly all of his 80-grade power in games. He doesn't walk a lot or play defense well, but if you can hit for as much average and power as Jiménez does, it doesn't matter a whole lot.

Luis Robert looked like an emerging superstar early on in the majors. Last year's No. 6 prospect showed enormous power and Gold Glove defense in his debut, and at times flashed enough hit tool and plate approach to hold up as the total package. At other times, contact completely eluded him; he hit .137 with a 34 percent strikeout rate in September. Robert will need to make adjustments, especially against same-side pitching, but all-in-all there were more positives than negatives to take away from his debut.

Dylan Cease was quite a prospect in his own right, topping out at No. 26 on the 2019 Top 101. He has struggled to throw strikes in the majors, and struggled to fool batters as well in 2020, leading to a 7.36 DRA lurking behind his superficially impressive 4.01 ERA. Cease's stuff is too good to be this bad, but we're starting to think about wanting to see what this looks like in relief again.

Nomar Mazara is somehow still eligible for this list as well. Our 2016 No. 5 prospect sure looks like he peaked before he ever hit the majors. He's heading towards a non-tender this winter after the White Sox failed to kickstart his stalled offensive development.

Part 3: Featured Articles

White Sox All-Time Top 10 Players

by Rob Mains

POSITION PLAYERS

RAY SCHALK, C (1912–1928)
Although a below-average hitter, Schalk played 1,727 games at catcher, the most in baseball history when he retired and still eighteenth on the all-time list. A slight man, listed at 5'9", 165 but probably a couple inches shorter and ten pounds lighter, he won accolades for his all-around defense, mobility, and ability to handle a pitching staff that included spitballers and knuckleballers. For years he held the record for stolen bases by a catcher, 30, set in 1916, and he still holds the record for career assists and double plays at the position.

EDDIE COLLINS, 2B (1915–1926)
He came to the White Sox in a salary dump trade after winning the MVP with the A's in 1914. He was already 28 when he joined the team but was an excellent hitter, fielder, and baserunner through his 30s, averaging .331/.426/.424 and leading the league in stolen bases three times. He was in the top ten in the league for batting nine times and on-base twelve times and hit .409 in the team's 1917 World Series win over the Giants, its last until 2005. His batting average is the highest in franchise history and his on-base percentage second only to Frank Thomas's.

NELLIE FOX, 2B (1950–1963)
The indestructible second baseman—he missed just 20 games in the 11 years from 1952 to 1962—known for the choked-up grip and big chaw of tobacco had 2,470 hits for the White Sox, second to Appling. In the decade from 1951 to 1960, he hit .303 with a .363 on base percentage, averaging 190 hits and 94 runs per year, finishing first or second in the league in hits eight times, eight times leading the league in singles. He was the league's MVP in 1959 for the American League

champions, winning the second of his three Gold Gloves. He was the second great second baseman gifted to the Pale Hose by Connie Mack, although the Tall Tactician was sliding into senescence by 1949, so possibly it was his son Earle who undervalued Fox and overvalued the frequently inebriated catcher Joe Tipton.

ROBIN VENTURA, 3B (1989–1998)
Admit it: The first thing that comes to mind is his 1993 brawl with 46-year-old Nolan Ryan. That's OK. Just remember the five Gold Gloves, 171 homers (seventh in team history), 741 RBI (eighth), durability (45 missed games, total, from 1990 to 1998), his first-round pick in the 1988 draft, and his .409 average for the Olympic gold medal team that summer, too, OK?

GEORGE DAVIS, SS (1902–1909)
He jumped leagues, from the National League Giants to the American League White Sox in 1902, then back to the Giants, then back to the White Sox again. He spent the last eight years of his career, starting when he was 31, with the White Sox. He was the best position player on the club most of those years, a switch-hitter with an above-average bat and outstanding glove. He was the cleanup hitter for the 1906 World Champions. A late addition to the Hall of Fame (in 1998, almost 60 years after his death in obscurity), a rare example of the Veteran's Committee fulfilling an education function by elevating a player who should have been better remembered.

LUKE APPLING, SS (1930–1950)
From 1947 to 1949, he played in all but 42 of Chicago's games, hitting .307/.416/.387—in his forties. He holds the White Sox records for games, plate appearances, and hits despite missing 1944 and most of 1945 due to the war. He wasn't just an accumulator of stats; he won two batting titles and drew a ton of walks, finishing with a .310/.399/.398 batting line, all with the White Sox. Ironically, he was nicknamed "Old Aches and Pains" for his constant complaining about injuries and ailments—all while accumulating 600 or more plate appearances at the demanding shortstop position in eleven seasons, tied for seventh in league history to that point.

LUIS APARICIO, SS (1956–62, 1968–1970)
"Little Louie," the only Hall of Famer from Venezuela, was an outstanding fielder who led the league in stolen bases each of his first seven years in the majors (and the next two as well, after he was traded to the Orioles). He was a below-average hitter every year except his last in Chicago, when he fluked his way to a .313 batting average (hitting .265 in is other nine years with the club), but he added

value with his speed and his glove. The sparkplug for the 1959 league champion Go-Go Sox, he was second to Fox in the MVP vote. He won the Gold Glove seven times with the club.

FIELDER JONES, OF (1901–1908)
He jumped from the National League for the White Sox' inaugural season in 1901, was named the team's player-manager early in the 1904 season, and led the 1906 "Hitless Wonders" club to a World Series upset over the Cubs. An excellent center fielder (Fielder was his actual first name) who stole an average of 26 bases per year, his .269/.357/.326 batting line was better-than-average in the Deadball Era.

MINNIE MINOSO, LF (1951–1957, 1960–1961, 1964, 1976, 1980)
The three-way trade that brought him to Chicago cost the team two decent outfielders and was still a heist. Adjusted for ballpark and era, Thomas, Collins, and Minoso are the three best hitters in franchise history. He rarely missed a game, was an excellent fielder, led the league in triples and stolen bases twice and doubles and total bases once, hit 20 homers and drove in 100 runs four times, and hit .304/.397/.468. He's the only player in club history with more than 130 homers and stolen bases. He was also the first player of color on the club, arriving more than four years after Jackie Robinson joined the Dodgers. To date, these accomplishments have been insufficient to earn him a plaque in Cooperstown.

FRANK THOMAS, DH/1B (1990–2005)
Is there a better modern nickname than The Big Hurt? He holds the franchise records for homers (448), runs (1,327), RBI (1,465), walks (1,466), OPS (.995), and park- and season-adjusted OPS (61 percent above average). Between 1991 and 1997, he averaged a 1.056 OPS, 36 homers, and 118 RBI despite two strike-shortened years. He won back-to-back MVPs in 1993 and 1994 and was in the top eight in the vote for seven straight years. Tenth on the career list for walks draw, he had 10 seasons of 100 or more walks; only Lou Gehrig, Ted Williams, Babe Ruth, and Barry Bonds had more.

PITCHERS

DOC WHITE, LHP (1903–1913)
He completed a degree in dentistry from Georgetown, hence the nickname. He jumped from the Phillies to the White Sox after the 1902 season and the leagues agreed to stop raiding each other before he could jump back. He was one of the top pitchers in the league, with a 139-95 record and 2.08 ERA from 1903 to 1910, including a league-leading 1.52 ERA in 1906 and 27 wins the next year. His record of five straight shutouts at the end of the 1904 season stood until Don Drysdale

broke it in 1968. A sinkerballer, he threw hard enough to get an above-average number of strikeouts. Thus he was less dependent on his defenses than is typical of the breed.

ED WALSH, RHP (1904–1916)

Big Ed threw 464 innings in 1908, 422 1/3 in 1907, and 393 in 1912, the first-, third-, and fourth-most in American League history, but his most famous record is his 1.82 career ERA (1.81 with Chicago), the lowest ever. In 1908, the spitballer went 40-15 with a 1.42 ERA, starting 49 games, completing 42 of them, and relieving 17 (for which he's retroactively credited with six saves, most in the league). After averaging 361 innings per season from 1906 to 1912, his arm was shot, and he managed only 172.2 more innings in his last four years in Chicago.

EDDIE CICOTTE, RHP (1912–1920)

His career numbers would have been better had he not been, you know, kicked out of baseball for throwing the 1919 World Series. Cicotte was the first prominent knuckleball pitcher in the game. In his nine years with the club, he was 156-101 with a 2.25 ERA, including 29-12, 1.53 in 1917 and 29-7, 1.82 in 1919. He was a workhorse, averaging over 300 innings in each of his last four seasons. His moment of poor judgment doesn't erase the fact that he was a dominating pitcher who was almost impossible to homer off of, even by the standards of the Deadball Era.

RED FABER, RHP (1914–1933)

One of the last legal spitball pitchers, Farber was relatively late to the majors. He signed with the Pirates but they sold him after he hurt is arm in a distance-throwing contest in 1914. He was 25 when he joined the White Sox in 1916. His best years immediately followed the Black Sox scandal; from 1920 to 1922, he won 69 games, 21 or more per year, with a league-best 2.76 ERA. He remained in the club's rotation until he was in his 40s, and over his 20-year career, all with Chicago, he compiled a 3.15 ERA and a 254-213 record despite pitching for only seven teams that won more games than they lost.

TED LYONS, RHP (1923–1946)

Lyons is the franchise leader in innings, 4,161, and wins, 260. His totals would've been higher but for his service with the Marines in 1942-44. His nickname, "Sunday Teddy," refers to him being a once-a-week pitcher beginning in 1935. In 1927 and 1930, though, he led the league in innings and complete games. He played his entire career for the White Sox, leading the league with a 2.10 ERA in 1942, when he was 41. Still indefatigable, that year he started 20 games and completed 20.

THORNTON LEE, LHP (1937–1947)

Lee was a 30-year-old with a 4.51 ERA over parts of four seasons when the White Sox acquired him for almost nothing after the 1936 season. Helped by a correction to his mechanics by coach/ex-catcher Muddy Ruel, over the next five years, he led American League lefties in starts, innings, and wins, with a 3.35 ERA. In his best year, 1941, he was 22-11 (credited with nearly 30 percent of the team's 77 wins) with a league-leading 2.37 ERA and 30 complete games. He was sidelined by injuries over much of the next three seasons but returned in 1945 for a strong campaign, going 15-12 with a 2.44 ERA.

BILLY PIERCE, LHP (1949–1961)

Pierce was traded to the White Sox for catcher Aaron Robinson, who caught 211 games for the Tigers, while Pierce was the Sox' best starter during the 1950s. He's fourth in franchise history for innings, starts, and wins, and fifth in era-adjusted ERA. Listed at 5'10", he became one of the league's most durable pitchers, leading the league in complete games three straight years, throwing at least 171 innings every season with the club, and leading the league with a 1.97 ERA in 1955. That season, the league-average ERA was more than twice as high.

WILBUR WOOD, LHP (1967–1978)

Wood had one of the weirder careers in history. He bounced between the minors and majors over seven seasons with two organizations before a trade to the White Sox after the 1966 season. He learned to throw a knuckleball after the trade. Over the next four years, he was the hardest-working reliever in baseball, averaging 71 games and 111 innings per year. The White Sox moved him to the rotation in 1971, and he took on ridiculous workloads, averaging 45 starts (leading the league four times) and 330 innings from 1971-1975, averaging a 21-18 record and 3.08 ERA. Early in 1976, a line drive shattered his kneecap, and he never recovered, managing only 347 innings over the last three years of his career.

MARK BUEHRLE, LHP (2000–2011)

His 11 straight seasons of 200-plus innings pitched for the Sox is the most in the majors since Steve Carlton pitched 13 straight from 1968 to 1980. And he wasn't a mere innings-eater; he was among the top ten in the league in wins and ERA four times each. He had a 161-119 record with the team and 3.83 ERA that was 20 percent better than average. He was also a fine fielder, picking up Gold Gloves his last two years with team, and pitched a perfect game in 2009.

CHRIS SALE, LHP (2010–2016)

Sale and Buehrle are the only pitchers on this list who threw a pitch since Jimmy Carter was President. Of course, you know him; five straight top-six Cy Young Award finishes, from 2012 to 2016, will do that. During those years, he led the league in ERA (3.06), lowest OPS allowed (.635), strikeouts to walks (5.1), and aesthetically unpleasing collared throwback uniforms destroyed (several).

A Taxonomy of 2020 Abnormalities

by Rob Mains

I'm going to start this with a trivia question. Trust me, it's relevant. Don't bother skipping to the end of the article to find the answer, it's not there.

Only five players have appeared in 140 or more games for 16 straight seasons. Who are they?

It's a trivia question starting off an essay, so you know how this works: Whatever you guessed, you're wrong. It's okay. As someone who purchased this book, chances are good that you're an educated baseball fan. But the circumstances behind 2020 force us to abandon, or at least seriously question, some of our favorite patterns and crutches for evaluating the game we love.

We just completed what was undoubtedly the strangest season in MLB history. No fans, geographically limited schedule, universal DH, seven-inning twin bills, runners on second in extra innings, a 16-team postseason, a club playing at a Triple-A stadium. Some of these changes will likely persist (sorry), but we've never had so many tweaks dumped on us all at once, at least not since they figured out how many balls were in a walk.

And the biggest, of course, was the 60-game season. The 19th century was dotted with teams that went bankrupt before the season ended, but the lone season with only 60 scheduled games was 1877. That year there were only six teams, the league rostered a total of 77 players (just 16 more than the 2020 Marlins), and batters called for pitches to be thrown high or low by the pitcher, who was 50 feet away. We can say the 2020 season was easily the shortest ever for recognizable baseball.

As such, it'll stand out. Few abbreviated seasons do. Just about everybody reading this knows the 1994 season ended after Seattle's Randy Johnson struck out Oakland's Ernie Young for the last out of the Mariners-A's game on August 11. The ensuing player strike wiped out the rest of the season and the postseason. Teams played only 112-117 games that year.

And many of you know that a strike in the middle of the 1981 season split the season in two, resulting in the only Division Series until 1995. Teams played only 103-111 games that year, the shortest regular season since 1885.

Those two seasons are memorable. So when we see that nobody drove in 100 runs in 1981, or that Greg Maddux was the only pitcher with 180 or more innings pitched in 1994, we think, "Of course. Strike year."

But we don't remember other short years. You might not recall that the 1994 strike spilled into the next year, chopping 18 games off the 1995 schedule. You might've read that the 1918 season, played during the last pandemic, ended after Labor Day due to the government's World War I "work or fight" order. A strike erased the first week and a half of the 1972 season, but that year's best known as the last time pitchers batted in the American League.

The point is, while we don't remember small changes to the schedule, we remember the big ones. The 1981 mid-season strike. The 1994 season- and Series-ending strike. And, of course, the pandemic-shortened 2020 season. We won't need a reminder why Marcell Ozuna's 18 homers were the fewest to lead the National League in a century. (Literally; Cy Williams led with 15 in 1920.)

Now, about that trivia question. The five players are Hank Aaron, Brooks Robinson, Pete Rose, Ichiro Suzuki, and Johnny Damon. The one nobody gets, of course, is Damon, and a lot of people miss Ichiro, whose last season of 140-plus games came garbed in the red-orange and ocean blue of Miami when he was 42. That's half of what makes it a good question. The other half is the two guys whom many think made the list but didn't. Lou Gehrig? His streak started in the Yankees' 42nd game of the 1925 season and lasted only 13 seasons after that. And everybody assumes Cal Ripken Jr. did it, having played 2,632 straight games over 17 seasons. But one of those 17 seasons was 1994, when the Orioles played only 112 games.

My point? *I just told you* everybody remembers the 1994 strike year, but everybody forgets it fell in the middle of Ripken's streak, separating the first twelve years from the last four. Just because we recall something doesn't mean it's always at the front of our minds.

Nobody is going to forget 2020, and baseball is obviously not the main reason. But there will come a time in the future when you're looking at a player's or a team's record, and there will be baffling numbers there for 2020, and you'll think, "I wonder what happened." (Not to mention the missing line for minor league players.) Just like you forgot that the 1994 strike limited Ripken to 112 games.

Try not to forget it, though. The 2020 season resulted in weird statistical results for several reasons.

There were only 60 games.
I know, duh. But that had impacts beyond counting stats like Ozuna's home run total or Yu Darvish and Shane Bieber leading the majors with eight wins. (I know, pitcher wins, but still.)

The 162-game season is the longest among major North American sports, and that duration gives us a gift. Over the course of a long season, small variations tend to even out. A player who has a ten-game hot streak will probably have a ten-game cold streak. A team that starts the year losing a bunch of close games will probably win a bunch of them. We get regression to the mean. Statistics stabilize.

Consider flipping a coin. Over the long run, we expect it to come up heads about half the time. But the fewer flips, the more variation there'll be. If you flip a coin six times, probability theory tells us you'll get at least two-third heads about 34 percent of the time. Flip it 30 times, your chance of two-thirds heads drops to five percent.

Or, relevant to this case, if you flip a coin 60 times, your chance of getting at least 36 heads—that's 60 percent—is 7.75 percent. Expand the coin-flipping to 162 times, and the chance of getting 60 percent heads drops to 0.73 percent.

In other words, the odds of an outcome that's 20 percent better (or worse) than expected is *more than ten times higher* when you flip your coin 60 times than when you do it 162 times. Call it small sample size, call lack of mean reversion, or call it luck not evening out, 162 is a lot more predictive than 60. You get much more variation over 60 games than over 162. Bieber's 1.63 ERA and 0.87 FIP aren't something we'd see over a full season, and neither is Javier Baéz's .203/.238/.360.

Some players' lines in 2020 look normal. Brian Anderson had an .811 OPS in 2019 and an .810 OPS in 2020. (He probably would have gotten that last point if he'd been given enough time.) But there are many like Bieber and Baéz, some of them from young players still establishing their talent levels. The answer to the question, "What went right or wrong for that guy in 2020?" is most likely "Nothing, it was just a 2020 thing."

Preseason training was abbreviated for hitters.

Every year, spring training drags. Players get tired of it, fans get tired of it, and you sure can tell sportswriters get tired of it. Yes, something to get everyone into shape is necessary, but does it really have to drag on for over a month? Can't we shorten it?

The 2020 season answered in the negative, at least for hitters. Warren Spahn is credited with saying that hitting is timing and pitching is upsetting timing. It appears nobody had his timing down after the abbreviated July summer camp. Through August 9—18 games into the season—MLB batters were hitting .230/.311/.395 with a .275 BABIP. That BABIP, had it held, would have been the lowest since 1968, the Year of the Pitcher. In recent years it's hovered around .300.

It didn't hold. Play returned to more normal levels the rest of the year: .249/.325/.425 with a .297 BABIP starting August 10. But batters whose play concentrated in those first two weeks wound up with ugly lines. Andrew

Benintendi went on the injured list with a season-ending rib cage strain on August 11. His final line: .103/.314/.128 in 14 games. Franchy Cordero went on the IL with a hamate bone fracture on August 9 and a .154/.185/.231 line. Even though he came back strong in a late September return, it was too late to repair his full-season numbers.

Preseason training was abbreviated for pitchers.
Every year, spring training drags. Players get tired of it, fans get tired of it ... wait, I already said that. But the abbreviated preseason was tough on pitchers, too. As noted, they had the upper hand coming out of the gate. But then they lost that hand. And then their arms, too.

The 2020 season was spread over 67 days. During those 67 days, 237 pitchers hit the Injured List, compared to 135 in the first 67 days of 2019. A lot of those IL stints, though, were COVID-19-related. Still, over the first 67 days of the 2019 season, there were 72 pitchers on the IL with arm injuries. That figure jumped to 110 in 2020, a 53 percent increase.

There are a number of factors contributing to pitcher arm injuries, ranging from usage to velocity, but it appears that attenuated preseason training played a role. A lot of pitchers had super-short seasons due to arm woes. Corey Kluber, Roberto Osuna, and Shohei Ohtani combined for seven innings, none after August 8. All suffered arm injuries. We'll never know whether they'd have fared better with a longer preseason, but we can guess how they probably feel.

Everybody played.
Rosters were set to expand from 25 to 26 in 2020, so even if we'd had a normal season, we'd have likely seen 2019's record of 1,410 players on MLB rosters broken. But due to the pandemic, rosters started the year at 30 and were cut to only 28. Add multiple COVID-19 absences and the revolving door caused by poor starts by hitters and a rash of pitcher arm injuries, and 1,289 players appeared in MLB games in 2020. The comparable figure over the first 67 days of the 2019 season was 1,109. That 16 percent increase works out to an average of six more players per team in 2020 compared to a similar slice of 2019. A future look back at 2020 rosters will include a lot of unfamiliar names.

Plus became a minus.
In advanced metrics, we adjust batter and pitcher performance for park and league/era variations. A plus sign appended to the end of a measure means that it's adjusted for park and league. It's scaled to an average of 100, with higher figures above average and lower figures below average. (Similarly, a metric with a minus is also park- and league-adjusted and scaled to 100, with lower values better.) Here at BP, our advanced measure of offensive performance is DRC+. Baseball-Reference has OPS+ and FanGraphs has wRC+.

Using park and league adjustments, we can compare Dante Bichette's 1995 Steroid Era season at pre-humidor Coors Field (.340/.364/.620, 40 homers, 128 RBI, MVP runner-up) with Jim Wynn's 1968 Year of the Pitcher season at the cavernous Astrodome (.269/.376/.474, 26 homers, 67 RBI, no MVP votes). It's not close. DRC+, OPS+, and wRC+ all give the nod to Wynn, handily. This is a useful tool. As my Baseball Prospectus colleague Patrick Dubuque tweeted last fall, "Please note that when I ask how you are, I am already adjusting for era."

The 2020 season messes up plus (and minus) stats for two reasons. First, the park adjustment was based on only 30 home games instead of the usual 81. Everything noted above regarding the short season applies, literally doubly, to park effect calculations. DRC+ uses a single-season park factor. OPS+ uses a three-year average and wRC+ five years. The figure for 2020 is suspect.

Second, OPS+ and wRC+ adjust for league: American and National. (DRC+ adjusts for opponent, regardless of league.) While there were two leagues in 2020, they were an artificial construct. To reduce travel, teams played opponents geographically, not based on league. There weren't two leagues, American and National. There were three, Western, Central, and Eastern.

That makes a difference because teams in the same league played in different run-scoring environments. AL teams scored 4.58 runs per game, NL teams 4.71. That's a small difference. But teams in the East scored 0.21 more runs per game (4.95) than teams in the West (4.74), and they both scored a lot more than Central teams (4.25). Adjusting for league misses that difference, so this book will be safe in that regard, but other sources may be distorted somewhat.

Not every game was a "game."

In 2020, the rising tide of strikeouts was finally stemmed. Strikeouts per team per game fell from 8.8 in 2019 to 8.7 in 2020. That marked the first decline after 14 straight annual increases.

In 2020, the rising tide of strikeouts rose higher. Batters struck out in 23.4 percent of plate appearances compared to 23.0 percent in 2019. That marked the 15th straight annual increase.

Both are true statements.

Because of two rule changes—seven-inning doubleheaders and runners on second in extra innings—games in 2020 were unprecedented in their brevity. There were 37.0 plate appearances per game in 2020. The only years with fewer were 1904 and 1906-1909. The average game in 2020 entailed 8.61 innings pitched, the fewest since 1899.

So when you see any per-game stats for 2020, you need to increase them by 3 or 4 percent to get them on equal footing with recent years.

Or, better, just ignore them. Last year happened. There were major league games contested between major league teams. But when you're looking at those physical or electronic baseball cards, when you're weaving narratives over why this young player's inevitable rise to stardom fell apart or why that old veteran rekindled his magic, don't linger on the 2020 line. It was just too weird.

Thanks to Lucas Apostoleris for research assistance.

—Rob Mains is an author of Baseball Prospectus.

Tranches of WAR

by Russell A. Carleton

We ask "replacement level" to be a lot of things. Sometimes contradictory things. Sometimes I wonder if we know what it even means anymore. The original idea was that it represented the level of production that a team could expect to get from "freely available talent", including bench players, minor leaguers, and waiver wire pickups. It created a common benchmark to compare everyone to, and for that reason, it represented an advancement well beyond what was available at the time. In fact, it created a language and a framework for evaluating players that was not just better but *entirely* different than what came before it.

But then we started mumbling in that language. The idea behind "wins above replacement" was one part sci-fi episode and one part mathematical exercise. Imagine that a player had disappeared before the season and suddenly, in an alternate timeline, his team would have had to replace him. The distance between him and that replacement line was his value. We need to talk about that alternate timeline.

Without getting too into 2:00 am "deep conversations" with extensive navel-gazing, it's worth thinking about why one player might not be playing, while another might.

- A player might not be playing because he has a short-term injury or his manager believes that he needs a day off.
- A player might not be playing because he has a longer-term injury that requires him to be on the injured list.

There's a difference here between these two situations. In particular, the first one generally *doesn't* involve a compensatory roster move, while the second one does. It's possible, though not guaranteed, that the person who will be replacing the injured/resting player would be the same in either case. That matters. Teams generally carry a spare part for all eight position players on the diamond, although in the era of a four-player bench, those spare parts usually are the backup plan for more than one spot.

Chicago White Sox 2021

A couple of years ago, I posed a hypothetical question. Suppose that a team had two players in its system fighting for a fourth outfielder spot. One of them was a league average hitter, but would be worth 20 runs below average if allowed to play center field for a full season. One of them was a perfectly average fielder, but would be 15 runs below average as a hitter, if allowed to play an entire season. Which of the two should the team roster? It's tempting to say the second one, as overall, he is the better player. That misses the point. A league average hitter on the bench isn't just a potential replacement for an injured outfielder. He might also pinch hit for the light-hitting shortstop in a key spot. You keep the average hitter on the roster, even though he isn't a hand-in-glove fit for one specific place on the field, because being a bench player is a different job description than being a long-term fill-in for someone. If you find yourself in need of a longer-term fill-in, you can bring the other guy up from AAA.

When we're determining the value of an everyday player though, if he had disappeared before the season and a team would have had to replace his production, they likely would have done it with a player who was a long-term fill-in type because they would have had to replace a guy who played everyday. Maybe that's the same guy that they would have rostered on their bench anyway, but we don't know. It gets to the query of what we hope to accomplish with WAR. Are we looking for an accurate modeling of reality or are we looking for a common baseline to compare everyone to? Both have their uses, but they are somewhat different questions.

Let's talk about another dichotomy.

- A player might not be playing because he isn't very good and is a bench-level player.
- A player might not be playing because there is another player on the team who has a situational advantage that makes him the better choice today. The classic case of this is a handedness platoon. On another day, he might be a better choice.

When we think about player usage, I think we're still stuck in the model that there are starters and there are scrubs. We have plenty of words for bench players or reserves or backups or utility guys. We do still have the word "platoon" in our collective vocabulary, but in the age of short benches, it's hard to construct one. It's always been hard to construct them. You have to find two players who hit with different hands, have skill sets that complement each other, and probably play the same position. In the era of the short bench, one of them had probably better double as a utility player in some way. Baseball has a two-tiered language geared toward the idea of regulars and reserves. The fact that it was so easy for me to find plenty of synonyms for "a player whose primary function is to come into a game to replace a regular player if he is injured or resting" should tell you something.

I'm always one to look for "unspoken words" in baseball. What is it called when someone is both half of a platoon and the utility infielder? That guy exists sometimes, but he reveals himself in that role—usually by accident. We don't have a word for that, and whenever I find myself saying "we don't have a word for that", I look for new opportunities. What do you call it, further, when the job of being the utility infielder is decentralized across the whole infield with occasional contributions from the left fielder? It's not even a "super-utility" player. What happens when you build your entire roster around the idea that everyone will be expected to be a triple major?

⚾ ⚾ ⚾

I think someone else beat me to this one, and on a grand scale. Platoons work because we know that hitters of the opposite hand to the pitcher get better results than hitters of the same hand, usually to the tune of about 20 points of OBP. If you want to express that in runs, it usually comes out to somewhere around 10 to 12 runs of linear weights value prorated across 650 PA. But hang on a second, now let's say that we have two players who might start today, both of roughly equal merit with the bat. One has a handedness advantage, but is the worse fielder of the two. In that case, as long as his "over the course of a season" projection as a fielder at whatever position you want to slot him into is less than a 10-run drop from the guy he might replace, then he's a better option today.

We're not used to thinking of utility players as bat-first options, who would play below-average defense at three different infield positions. That guy might hook on as a 2B/3B/LF type (Howie Kendrick, come on down!) but teams usually think to themselves that they need as their utility infielder someone who "can handle" shortstop, the toughest of the infield spots to play. If someone can do that *and* hit well, he's probably already starting somewhere, so he's not available as a utility infielder. It's easier for those glove guys to find a job. In a world where the replacement for a shortstop *has to be* the designated utility infielder, that makes sense.

But as we talked about last week, we're living in a different world. The rate at which a replacement for a regular starter turns out to be *another starter* shifting over to cover has gone way up over the last five years. There was always some of it in the game, but this has been a supernova of switcheroos. Now if your second baseman is capable of playing a decent shortstop, that 2B/3B/LF guy can swap in. He's not actually playing shortstop, and maybe the defense suffers from the switch, but if he's got enough of a bat, he might outhit those extra fielding miscues. And in doing so, he is effectively your backup shortstop.

Somewhere along the lines, teams got hip to the idea of multi-positional play from their regulars. I've written before about how you can't just put a player, however athletic, into a new position and expect much at first. The data tell us that. Eventually, players can learn to be multi-positionalists, but it takes time, roughly on the order of two months, before they're OK. But there's a hidden message in there. If you give a player some reps at a new spot, he's a reasonably gifted athlete and somewhat smart and willing to learn, he could probably pick it up enough to get to "good enough," and it doesn't take forever. You just have to be purposeful about it. Maybe you get to the point where you can start to say "he's still below average but we could move him there and get another bat into the lineup, and it's a net win."

Teams have started to build those extra lessons into their player development program. It used to be seen as a mark of weakness to be relegated to "utility player" because that meant that you were a bench player (all those synonyms above come with a side of stigma). Now, it's a way of building a team. If you get a few reps in the minors (where it doesn't count) at a spot, you'll have at least played the spot at game speed before. There are limits to how far you can push that. A slow-footed "he's out in left field because we don't have the DH" guy is never going to play short, but maybe your third baseman can try second base and not look like a total moose out there.

⚾ ⚾ ⚾

Back to WAR. I'd argue that the world of starters and scrubs is slowly disintegrating, for good cause. In the event that a regular starter really does go down with an injury–ostensibly, the alternate universe scenario that WAR is attempting to model–it makes the team a little more resilient to replacing him. And the good news is that you're more likely to be able to replace him with the best of the bench bunch, rather than the third-best guy, because the best guy doesn't have to be an exact positional match for the guy who got hurt. And that's what the manager would want to do. He'd want to replace that long-term production, not with an amalgam of everyone else who played that position, but with the best guy available from his reserves.

Now this is still WAR. We still want to retain the principle that we should be measuring a player, and not his teammates. We need some sort of common baseline, and despite what I just said, we'll still need some sort of amalgam. To construct that, I give to you the idea of the tranche. The word, if you've not heard it before, refers to a piece of a whole that is somehow segmented off. It's often used in finance to talk about layers of a financial instrument.

Here, I want you to consider that there are 30 starters at each of the seven non-battery positions (catchers should have their own WAR, since only a catcher can replace a catcher). We can identify them by playing time, and we can futz around with the definition a little bit if we need to. Next, among those who aren't in that starting pool, we identify the top tranche of the 30 best bench players, which I would again identify by playing time, and then the second and third and fourth and so on. If a player were to disappear, his manager would probably want to take a guy from that top tranche of the bench to replace him. In a world where even the starters can slide around the field, that becomes more feasible.

We can take a look at that top tranche and say "How many of them showed that they are able to play (first, second, etc.)?" and therefore could have directly substituted for the starter? How many of them could have been a direct substitute for our injured player? We don't know whether one of them would be on *a specific* team, but we can say that 40 percent of the time, a manager would have been able to draw from tranche 1 in filling the role, and 35 percent from tranche 2. But on tranche 1, we can also look at how many of those players played a position that could have then shifted and covered for that spot. We'd need some eligibility criteria for all of this (probably a minimum number of games played) but it would just be a matter of multiplication. Shortstop would be harder to fill, and managers would probably be dipping a little further down in the talent pool, and so replacement level would be lower, as it is now.

Doing some quick analysis, I found that the difference in just batting linear weights (haven't even gotten into running or fielding) between tranche 1 and tranche 2 in 2019 was about 6.5 runs, prorated across 650 PA. Between tranche 1 and tranche 3, it's 10.8 runs. The ability to shift those plate appearances up the ladder has some real value.

This part is important. We can also give credit to starters for the positions that they showed an ability to play, even if they didn't play them (this is the guy fully capable of playing center, but who's in a corner because the team already has a good center fielder) because he allows a team to carry a player who hits like a left fielder to functionally be the team's backup center fielder. He facilitates that movement upward among the tranches. We can start to appreciate the difference between a left fielder who would never be able to hack it in center (and the compensatory move that his team would have to make) and the left fielder who could do it, but just didn't have to very often.

Past that, you can continue to use whatever hitting and fielding and running metrics you like to determine a player's value, but when we get down to constructing that baseline, I'd argue we need a better conceptual and mathematical framework. It's going to require some more #GoryMath than we're used to, but I'd argue it's a better conceptualization of the way that MLB actually plays the game in 2020. If…y'know…MLB plays in 2020. If WAR is going to be our flagship statistic among the *acronymati*, then we need to acknowledge that it contains some old and starting-to-be-out-of-date assumptions about the game. We may need to tinker with it. Here's my idea for how. ■

—*Russell A. Carleton is an author of Baseball Prospectus.*

Secondhand Sport

by Patrick Dubuque

Back before time stopped, I liked to go to thrift stores. Now that I'm older, I rarely ever buy anything—I don't need much in my life, now—but I still enjoy the old familiar circuit: check to see if there are baseball cards to write about, look for board or card games to play with the kids, scan for random ironic jerseys, hit the book section. It takes ten, maybe fifteen minutes. Thrift stores are the antithesis of modern online shopping, because you don't know what they have, and you don't even really know what you want. It's junk, literal junk, stuff other people thought was worthless. That's what makes it great.

In an idealized economy, thrift stores shouldn't exist. Everybody has a living wage, and every product has a durability that exactly matches its desired life; nothing should need to be given away, no one should need to be given to. But then, thrift stores shouldn't work on a customer experience level, either. You wouldn't think an ethos of "let's make everything disorganized and hard to find" would lead to customer satisfaction, but low-budget retailers like TJ Maxx and Ross thrive on this model. People like bargain hunting as much for the hunting as the bargain; it's part of the experience, spending time as if it's a wager. There's a thrill, occasionally, in inefficiency.

In sports, the modern overuse of the word "inefficiency" is a condemnation: It insinuates that there is *an* efficiency, a correct way to be found, and that all other ways are wrong ways. It's prevalent in baseball but hardly contained to it; the lifehack, the Silicon Valley disruption are other examples of productivity creep in our daily lives. Their modern success makes plenty of sense. Maximization of resources, after all, is its own puzzle, and an industry of European board games is founded upon it. It's fun to take a system and optimize it, unravel it like a sudoku puzzle. If there's only one kind of genius, after all, there's no way anyone can fail to appreciate it.

Baseball has been hacking away at these perceived inefficiencies since its inception: platoons, bullpens, farm systems were all installed to extract more out of the tools at hand. But it's been a particular badge of the sabermetric movement, from Ken Phelps and his All-Star Team to Ricardo Rincon and the darlings of *Moneyball*. It's business, but it's also an ethos: the idea that there's treasure among the trash, something we all failed to appreciate until someone brought it to light.

It's the myth that made Sidd Finch so enticing, that fuels so many "best shape" narratives and new pitch promises. We all, athletes and unathletic sportswriters, want to believe that there's genius trapped inside us, and that it's just a matter of puzzling out the combination to unlock it. That our art, our style is the next inefficiency, waiting for our own Billy Beane. It's why we root for underdogs, and why we're excited for the Mike Tauchmans and the Eurubiel Durazos, champions of skin-deep mediocrity.

Except we aren't anymore, really. The days of "Free X" have descended beyond the ring of irony and into obscurity. There are still Xs to be freed, or at least one X, duplicated endlessly: Mike Ford, Luke Voit, Max Muncy. The undervalued one-dimensional slugger demonstrated how the game hasn't quite culturally caught up to its logical extreme. But for those who don't fit the rather spacious mold, times are grimmer. As Rob Arthur revealed several months ago, there's been a marked increase in the number of sub-replacement relievers. It's the outcome of a greater number of teams forced to play out games without the talent to win them, but it's also emblematic of the modern tendency of teams to dispose of their disposable assets, burning through cost-controlled arms the way that man chopped down forests in *The Lorax*. Stuff just isn't built to outlive their original owners anymore.

It's unsurprising, given how well-mined the market for inefficiencies has been of late. The disciples of the early analytics departments, and the disciples of those, have proliferated the league, with only a few backwater holdouts. The league has grown smarter, but every team has learned the same lesson. In fact, the phenomenon creates a peculiar kind of feedback loop: As teams value a specific subset of players or skills, prospective athletes learn to increase their own marketability by conforming themselves to the demands of their prospective employers.

And that's tragic, in the way that the extinction of animals is tragic; a certain amount of biodiversity in baseball has been lost. Shortstops hit like outfielders. Pitchers don't hit at all. Only the catchers remain idiosyncratic, thanks to the defensive demands of their position; eventually they too will be required to produce like everyone else, or they'll meet the fate of their battery mates. A perfect economy requires perfect production.

I mentioned earlier that more and more, I leave thrift stores empty-handed. It is true that I am more discerning than in the past; my bookshelves are full, and there are more streaming films than I will ever be able to watch. But there are other factors at play.

Thrift stores are, in a way, the bond markets of retail. When the economy is rough and other retailers are struggling, more people look secondhand for their products. But as recently as last year, publications were noting a reversal of the trend: Companies like Goodwill and Savers were expanding despite a strong economy. Publications credited a heightened sense of environmentalism and a rejection of cutting-edge fashion as drivers behind the increase, though the more likely answer is the modern American economy hasn't showered its favors equally, particularly among the young.

But it is more than just the economy. Baseball and thrift stores share something else in common, evident in our current conversations about re-starting the sport: They live in the gray area between public service and private enterprise. Thrift stores provide affordable necessities to lower-class citizens, and collectibles and fashion for the middle-class. Because of the success of the latter, prices have gone up across the board. Especially in terms of clothing, the middle-class flight from fashion into vintage has instead carried the aftereffects of fashion, including its costs, into a territory where people just want clothes. But there's another factor in the rise of prices, in the form of the internet.

The Goodwills of the world have grown smarter, too, employing the internet to extract full value from their detritus. Ebay, similarly, has lost much of the charm it had as a new frontier around the turn of the century. Everything has a price point now; even individual taste is no match for the algorithm, because anything rare, no matter how niche its market, is a collectible to someone.

The internet has had the same effect on thrift stores that sabermetrics has had on baseball; its equivalent to OBP was the bar scanner. As detailed in Slate, the rise of second-party stores on eBay and Amazon birthed an entire industry of used-good salespeople, armed with PDAs and scanners, buying books for three dollars to sell online for five. The author, Michael Savitz, reports earning $60,000 by working nearly 80 hours a week; he makes it clear that this is not a vocation of his choosing. It's long hours, with no real creativity or individuality, skimming the cream off of a local establishment and flipping it to someone with a little more money on the other side of the country. And once the vocation exists, the obvious question arises: why wait to put the wares out on the shelves? Why allow value to exist at all?

Nothing is ruined. Thrift stores will continue to sell polo shirts and DVDs, and baseball will continue to exist and make or lose money, depending on who you believe. But as we continue to refine our knowledge, we lose something in the conquest for efficiency, a delight born out of the unknown. The problem isn't the efficiency itself; we can't blame the booksellers, or the people sweeping freeways to collect grams of platinum from damaged catalytic converters. The problem is a system that requires this sort of profit-skimming behavior in order to feed families (or, for corporations, maximize shareholder return).

In times like these, with the 2020 season on the brink and the collective bargaining agreement close behind, it can often feel like the current situation is untenable. It can't keep going like this, even if we don't know what to do about it. But as with thrift stores, there's an equally irresistible feeling that it *has* to keep going, that it would be unimaginable to not have this broken, amazing sport. Both industries exist on an invisible foundation of friction, of chaos and unpredictability, even as both see their foundations buffed down to a perfect, untouchable polish. But if COVID-19 and its financial ramifications do, as some have suggested, make it such that the baseball that returns is fundamentally different than the baseball that came before, perhaps this is the time to lean in, and change the game even more. Fix bunting. Make defense more difficult. Create viable, alternate strategies. Add some chaos back into baseball. It's fun when no one knows quite where things are.

—Patrick Dubuque is an author of Baseball Prospectus.

Steve Dalkowski Dreaming

by Steven Goldman

We dream of being a pitcher, of starring in the major leagues. Depending on your age and your sense of historical perspective, you might imagine yourself as Walter Johnson, throwing harder than anyone else—hitting more batters than anyone else, too, but always feeling bad about it. You could picture yourself as a Tom Seaver or a David Cone, with all the stuff in the world but still being cerebral about it, thinking about so much more than burning 'em in there. There are so many models one could choose: You could be a Lefty Gomez, Jim Bouton, or Bill Lee, skilled, but not taking the whole thing too seriously, or a Lefty Grove, Bob Gibson, or Steve Carlton, powerful but treating each start like a mission to be survived instead of a game to be enjoyed.

Very few would dream of being Steve Dalkowski, the former Baltimore Orioles prospect who died of COVID-19 last week at the age of 80. Yet, there is something just as noble in Dalkowski's negative accomplishments—and accomplishments is what they are—as there is in the precision-engineered pitching of a Greg Maddux. You have to be very good to be that bad. Dalkowski had all of the stuff of the greatest pitchers but none of the command; his story is not one of failing to conquer his limitations, but striving against one of the cruelest hands that fate or genetics or personality can deal us: A desire to achieve great things which is almost but not quite matched by the ability to meet that goal.

As with Johnson, Grove, Bob Feller, and the rest of the hard-throwing pitchers who played before the advent of modern radar guns, we have to take the word of the players and coaches who saw Dalkowski pitch as to his velocity. He was a hard-drinking, maximum-effort pitcher who, if their memories are to be believed, consistently threw over 100 miles per hour. His was the Maltese Fastball, the stuff that dreams are made of. The problem is that velocity without command and control is still a good distance from utility. Dalkowski was the most effective towel you could design for a fish, the sleekest bathing suit intended to be worn by an astronaut, but that doesn't mean he wasn't beautiful: We can appreciate a journey even if it doesn't end at the intended destination.

Whether because of sloppy mechanics he couldn't calm, an inability to understand that a consistent 98 in the strike zone would likely be more effective than a consistent 110 out of it, or all that beer, Dalkowski could never make the adjustments that pitchers like Feller and Nolan Ryan made before him, possibly because he had so far to go: Feller, who never pitched in the minors, came up at 17 and spent three years walking almost seven batters per nine innings before settling in at 3.8 beginning when he was 20. Ryan started out walking over six batters per nine but gradually improved as his long career played out; for him to go from 6.2 walks per nine with the 1966 Greenville Mets to 3.7 with the 1989 Texas Rangers represents a 40 percent reduction. An equivalent improvement by Dalkowski would still have left him walking over 11 batters per nine innings.

Dalkowski was like *The Room* of pitchers, a player so bad he became good again. Cal Ripken, Sr., who both played with and managed Dalkowski, recalled in a 1979 *Sporting News* "where are they now" piece the occasion when the pitcher crossed up his catcher and his fastball, "hit the plate umpire smack in the mask. The mask broke all to pieces and the umpire wound up in the hospital for three days with a concussion. If they ever had a radar gun in those days, I'll bet Dalkowski would have been timed at 110 miles an hour."

Signed by the Orioles out of New Britain High in Connecticut in 1957, Dalkowski was sent to Kingsport in the Appalachian League, where he pitched 62 innings. He allowed only 22 hits in 62 innings, or 3.2 per nine, a number with no equivalent in major league history (though Aroldis Chapman came close in 2014), and also struck out 121 (17.6 per nine) and walked 129 (18.7). He was also charged with 39 wild pitches. That June, one of his fastballs clipped a Dodgers prospect named Bob Beavers and carried away part of his ear. "The first pitch was over the backstop, the second pitch was called a strike, I didn't think it was," Beavers said last year. "The third pitch hit me and knocked me out, so I don't remember much after that. I couldn't get in the sun for a while, and I never did play baseball again." Former minor leaguer Ron Shelton based the *Bull Durham* pitcher Nuke LaLoosh on Dalkowski. And yet, to see him as a figure of fun, an amusing loser, is to misunderstand something unique and strange.

Dalkowski kept on posting some of the strangest lines in baseball history. Pitching for the Stockton Ports of the Class C California League in 1960, he struck out 262 and walked 262 in 170 innings. Yet, he did improve, especially after pitching for Earl Weaver at Elmira in 1962. Weaver had previously had Dalkowski at Aberdeen in 1959, but wasn't ready to grapple with him then. This time he was. "I had grown more and more concerned about players with great physical abilities who could not learn to correct certain basic deficiencies no matter how much you instructed or drilled them," he related in his autobiography, *It's What You Learn After You Know It All That Counts*. He got permission from the Orioles to give all of his players the Stanford-Binet IQ test. "Dalkowski finished in the 1 percentile in his ability to understand facts. Steve, it was said to say, had the ability to do everything but learn." [sic]

IQ tests are problematic diagnostic tools, so take Weaver's estimate of Dalkowski's mental capabilities with a grain of salt. What's important is that even if he got to the right answer by way of the wrong reason, Weaver had learned something valuable. His insight was to stop asking Dalkowski to learn new pitches and just let him get by with the two that he had. Were Dalkowski a prospect today, that would have been a no-brainer: Can't develop a third pitch? The bullpen is right over there, sir. Player development wasn't like that then, but Weaver, temporarily Dalkowski's mentor, could let him work with what he had. According to Weaver, the pitcher responded: "In the final 57 innings he pitched that season Dalkowski gave up 1 earned run, struck out 110 batters, and walked only 11." It's not true—as per the *Elmira Star-Gazette*, as of late July, Dalkowski had walked 71 in 106 innings and finished with 114 in 160 innings, which means Dalkowski's control actually faded at the end of the season rather than improved—but that doesn't mean it didn't happen in some sense, just that it didn't happen that way. Again, it's the journey, not the destination, and his ERA was 3.04 so *something* had gone right.

Also along the way: The next spring, Orioles manager Billy Hitchcock was rooting for Dalkowski to make the team as a long-man—maybe Weaver had gotten through to him. There were things out of Weaver's control, like the universe's twisted sense of humor: that March, Dalkowski's elbow went "twang."

You sometimes read that it was the Orioles' insistence on Dalkowski learning the curve that did him in, but even if they hadn't learned their lesson, the injury was probably just a coincidence: Dalkowski had thrown an incredible number of pitches over the previous few years. Still, it testifies to the dangers of trying to get what you want and risking the loss of what you had. Dalkowski tried to come back, but the 110-mph stuff was gone. A pitcher with no control and no stuff is…a civilian. What followed were years of vagabond living, arrests for drunkenness. There were Alcoholics Anonymous meetings, assistance from baseball alumni associations, but none of it took. From the 1990s until the time of his passing he dwelt in an assisted living facility, suffering from alcohol-related dementia. He'd been a heavy drinker since his teenage years. As with all those pitches per game, there was a price to be paid. You make choices on the journey and some of them are irrevocable. It's like a fairy tale: "Bite of poison apple? Don't mind if I do."

In the aforementioned *Sporting News* profile, Chuck Stevens, the head of the Association of Professional Ballplayers of America, a ballplayer charity, said, "I've got nothing against drinking. I do it myself sometimes. But, I don't condone common drunkenness. We went through lots of heartache and many dollars, but Dalkowski didn't want to help himself and we weren't going to keep him drunk." The journey is *un*like a fairy tale: No one will come along and kiss it better, not if they're busy forming judgments.

In the end, we are left with a sort of philosophical chicken/egg conundrum: Is failing to meet your goals evidence of unfulfilled potential or the lack of it? Isn't what you did by definition what you were capable of doing? Or could you have broken through to something better with the right help, the right lucky break? These are unanswerable questions, and how we try to answer them may say more about us than about the people we're judging.

No pitcher ever has it easy. *All* pitchers must work hard. *All* pitchers must refine their craft. It's almost never just about *stuff*. Dalkowski dreaming is no insult to the great pitchers who made it; from Pete Alexander to Max Scherzer, they have all earned their way up. And yet, if it is true that we can only do as much as we can do, then the journey would be more of an adventure, the ultimate triumph or defeat more noble, if like Dalkowski we lacked 100 percent of the confidence, the command, the self-possession, the commitment, the resistance to making bad decisions that so many great players possess—to be gloriously human. Or, to put it more succinctly, it would be fun to be able to throw as hard as any person ever has. Even if just for a moment, and even if nothing more came of it than that, no one could say you hadn't lived life to the fullest.

—*Steven Goldman is an author of Baseball Prospectus.*

A Reward For A Functioning Society

by Cory Frontin and Craig Goldstein

On July 5, Nationals reliever Sean Doolittle said in the middle of a press conference regarding the restart of Major League Baseball and what would later be known as summer camp, "sports are like the reward of a functioning society." This sentence was amidst a much longer, thoughtful reply about the societal and health conditions under which MLB players were being brought back. It's a very similar sentiment to one Jane McManus used on April 7, when she discussed the White House's meeting with sports commissioners. She said "sports are the effect of a functioning society—not the precursor."

Both versions of the same sentiment spoke to a laudable ideal in the context of a country that was not addressing a rampaging virus, and opting instead to bring sports back for the feeling of normalcy rather than the reality of it. "Priorities," as McManus said.

On Wednesday, the NBA's Milwaukee Bucks conducted a wildcat/political strike, refusing to come out for Game 5 of their playoff series against the Orlando Magic. The Magic refused to accept the forfeit, and shortly thereafter other playoff series were threatened by player strikes. Eventually the league moved to postpone that day's games, folding to players leveraging their united power.

The backdrop against which these actions took place was the shooting by police of Jacob Blake. Blake was shot in the back seven times by police, as he attempted to get into his vehicle. He managed to survive the assault, but is paralyzed from the waist down.

⚾ ⚾ ⚾

The step taken to walk out, first by the Milwaukee Bucks, then subsequently by other NBA, WNBA, and MLB teams, was a step toward upholding the virtue of the sentiment described by McManus and Doolittle. But that sentiment does not align with the broad history of sports in this and other countries, a history that contradicts the core of the idealistic statement.

Sports have been a significant part of American society for most of its existence, expanding in importance and influence in recent years. The idea that society was functioning in a way that was worthy of the reward of sports for most of that time is laughable. Much of America is not functioning and has not functioned for Black people, full stop. The oppressed people at the center of this political act by players, specifically Black players, in concert throughout the NBA and in fits and starts throughout Major League Baseball, have not known a society that functions for them rather than *because* of them.

Politics has been part of the sports landscape since the inception of sport, but for just about as long people have bemoaned its presence. Sports are to be an escape, it is said. An escape from what, though? A functioning society?

No, the presence of sports has never signified a cultural or political system that is on the up and up. Rather, the presence of sports *reflect and reinforce the society that produces them.*

⚾   ⚾   ⚾

The Negro Leagues were born out of societal dysfunction. The need for entirely separate leagues, composed of Black and Latino players barred from the Major Leagues because of racism? That is not a functioning society, and yet there were sports.

Even the integration of players from the Negro Leagues resulted in a transfer of power and wealth from Black-owned businesses and communities and into white ones, mirroring the dysfunction that had bled into every aspect of American society at the time. Japheth Knopp noted in the Spring 2016 Baseball Research Journal:

> The manner in which integration in baseball—and in American businesses generally—occurred was not the only model which was possible. It was likely not even the best approach available, but rather served the needs of those in already privileged positions who were able to control not only the manner in which desegregation occurred, but the public perception of it as well in order to exploit the situation for financial gain. Indeed, the very word integration may not be the most applicable in this context because what actually transpired was not so much the fair and equitable combination of two subcultures into one equal and more homogenous group, but rather the reluctant allowance—under certain preconditions—for African Americans to be assimilated into white society.

To understand the value of a movement, though, is not to understand how it is co-opted by ownership, but to know the people it brings together and what they demand. When Jackie Robinson—the player who demarcated the inevitability of the end of the Negro leagues—attended the March on Washington for Jobs and Freedom in 1963, he did so with his family and marched alongside the people. He stood alongside hundreds of thousands to fight for their common civil and labor rights. "The moral arc of the universe is long," many freedom fighters have echoed, "but it bends towards justice." The bend, it is less frequently said, happens when a great mass of people place the moral arc of the universe on their knee and apply force, as Jackie, his family, and thousands of others did that day.

⚾ ⚾ ⚾

Of course, taking the moral arc of the universe down from the mantle and bending it is not without risk. Perhaps the outsized influence of athletes is itself a mark of a dysfunctional society, but, nonetheless, hundreds of athletes woke up on Wednesday morning with the power to bring in millions of dollars in revenues. That very power, as we would come to find out, was matched with the equal and opposite power to *not* bring those revenues. That power, in hands ranging from the Milwaukee Bucks, to Kenny Smith in the *Inside the NBA* Studio, from the unexpected ally, Josh Hader, and his largely white teammates to the notably Black Seattle Mariners, would be exercised for a single demand: the end to state violence against Black people. Not unlike the March itself, it sat at the intersection of the civil rights of Black Americans and bold labor action. The March on Washington stood in the face of a false notion of integration—against an integration of extraction but not one of equality—and proposed something different. Just the same, the acts of solidarity of August 26, 2020 will be remembered in stark defiance of MLB's BLM-branded, but ultimately empty displays on opening weekend.

Bold defiance like this can never be without risk. By choosing to exercise this power, the Milwaukee Bucks took a risk. They risked vitriol and backlash from those they disagreed with. They risked fines or seeing their contracts voided, as a walkout like this is prohibited by their CBA. They risked forfeiting a playoff game, one that, as the No. 1 seed in the playoffs, they'd worked all year to attain. They didn't know how Orlando would respond. It wasn't clear that other teams throughout the league would follow suit in solidarity. And it wasn't known the league would accept these actions and moderately co-opt them by "postponing" games that would have featured no players.

If the league reschedules the games, some of the athletes' risk—their shared sacrifice—will be diminished, in retrospect. But they did not know any of that when they took that risk. And it is often left to athletes to take these risks when others in society won't, especially those of their same socioeconomic status and levels of influence.

It is athletes, specifically BIPOC athletes, that take them, though, because they live with the risk of being something other than white in this country every day. They are no strangers to the realities of police brutality. It seems incongruous then, to say that sports are a reward for a functioning society when we rely on athletes to lead us closer to being a functioning society. Luckily, our beloved athletes, WNBA players first and foremost among them, understand what sports truly are: a pipebender for the moral arc of the universe.

> —*Craig Goldstein is editor in chief of Baseball Prospectus. Cory Frontin is an author of Baseball Prospectus.*

Index of Names

Abreu, José 14
Adolfo, Micker 66
Anderson, Tim 16
Bummer, Aaron 38
Burdi, Zack 40
Burger, Jake 90
Cease, Dylan 42
Collins, Zack 66
Cordero, Jimmy 44
Crochet, Garrett 75, 85
Dalquist, Andrew 75, 88
Despaigne, Odrisamer 76
Dyson, Jarrod 68
Eaton, Adam 18
Encarnación, Edwin 20
Engel, Adam 22
Flores Jr., Bernardo 77
Foster, Matt 46
Fry, Jace 48
García, Leury 24
Giolito, Lucas 50
González, Gio 52
González, Luis 69
Grandal, Yasmani 26
Hendriks, Liam 54
Heuer, Codi 56, 88
Jiménez, Eloy 28
Kelley, Jared 77, 86
Keuchel, Dallas 58
Kopech, Michael 78, 85
Lambert, Jimmy 79, 89
López, Reynaldo 60
Lynn, Lance 62
Madrigal, Nick 30, 83
Marshall, Evan 64
Mendick, Danny 32
Mercedes, Yermín 70
Moncada, Yoán 34
Ramos, Bryan 90
Robert, Luis 36
Rodón, Carlos 80
Rutherford, Blake 71, 90
Sheets, Gavin 71
Stiever, Jonathan 81, 87
Thompson, Matthew 82, 89
Tucker, Preston 72
Vargas, Emilio 82
Vaughn, Andrew 73, 84
Williams, Nick 73
Zavala, Seby 74

For the Joy of Keeping Score

THIRTY81 Project is an ongoing graphic design project focused on the ballparks of baseball. Since being established in 2013, scorecards have been a fundemantal part of the effort. Each two-page card is uniquely ballpark-centric — there are 30 variants — and designed with both beginning and veteran scorekeepers in mind. Evolving over the years with suggestions from fans, broadcasters, and official scorers, the sheets are freely available to everyone as printable letter-size PDFs at the project webshop: www.THIRTY81Project.com

Download, Print, Score, Repeat ...

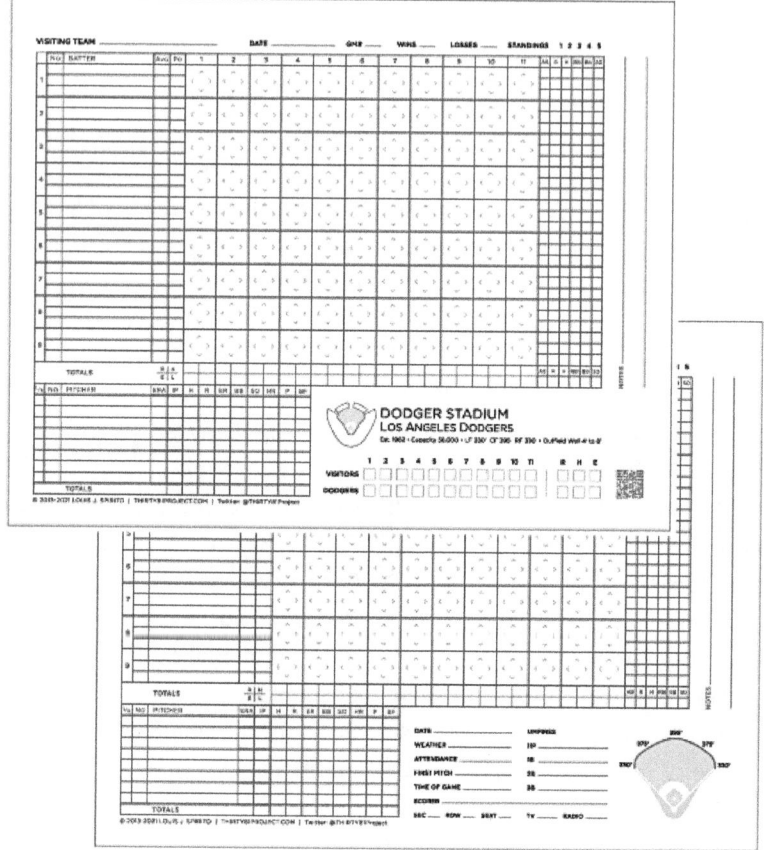

Scorecard design ©2013-2021 Louis J. Spirito | THIRTY81Project